The
Addictive
Personality

Also available from Harper/Hazelden

The Twelve Steps of Alcoholics Anonymous: Interpreted by the Hazelden Foundation, Hazelden

The Little Red Book, Hazelden

A.A.: The Story, Ernest Kurtz

Codependent No More, Melody Beattie

Is It Love or Is It Addiction?, Brenda Schaeffer

Holding Back: Why We Hide the Truth about Ourselves, Marie Lindquist

The Hazelden Meditation Series

Twenty-Four Hours a Day

The Promise of a New Day: A Book of Daily Meditations

Night Light: A Book of Nighttime Meditations

Each Day a New Beginning: Daily Meditations for Women

Touchstones: A Book of Daily Meditations for Men

Today's Gift: Daily Meditations for Families

Day by Day: Daily Meditations for Young Adults

Food for Thought: Daily Meditations for Dieters and Overeaters

The Love Book

Days of Healing, Days of Joy: Daily Meditations for Adult Children

One More Day: Daily Meditations for People with Chronic Illness

The Reflecting Pond: Meditations for Self-Discovery

Look to This Day: Twenty-Four Hours a Day for Everyone

The Addictive Personality

UNDERSTANDING
COMPULSION IN OUR LIVES

◆

1817

A Harper/Hazelden Book

Harper & Row, Publishers, San Francisco
Cambridge, Hagerstown, New York, Philadelphia, Washington
London, Mexico City, São Paulo, Singapore, Sydney

THE ADDICTIVE PERSONALITY: *Understanding Compulsion in Our Lives.* Copyright © 1988 by the Hazelden Foundation. This edition published by Harper & Row, Publishers, Inc., by arrangement with the Hazelden Foundation. All rights reserved. Printed in the United States of America. No part of this book may be used or reproduced in any manner whatsoever without written permission except in the case of brief quotations embodied in critical articles and reviews. For information address Harper & Row, Publishers, Inc., 10 East 53rd Street, New York, NY 10022.

FIRST HARPER & ROW EDITION PUBLISHED IN 1988.

Library of Congress Cataloging in Publication Data

Nakken, Craig.
   The addictive personality.

   "A Harper/Hazelden book."
   Includes index.
   1. Compulsive behavior.   I. Title.
RC533.N34   1988   616.85'227   88-45140
ISBN 0-06-255488-3

89   90   91   92   MUR   10   9   8   7   6   5

To my wife Jane and to Nature,
both of whom have taught me much
about myself, relationships,
beauty, and love

CONTENTS

Coping Breaks Down
Interacting Breaks Down
The Addict: Wanting to be Alone
The Self: Not Wanting to be Alone
Environmental Problems
Physical Signs of Breaking Down
Thoughts of Suicide
Stuck in Stage Three

INTRODUCTION

This book is written to help its readers better understand the process of addiction and the development of an addictive personality. It seeks to broaden people's minds about the depth and dimensions of one of the most widespread and costly illnesses facing us today. It is my intention to give the reader a better idea of addiction, understanding what it is people can get addicted to, and what happens inside the people who suffer from this illness.

In the past, the term "addiction" has had a very limited focus, being associated almost entirely with alcohol and other drugs. In reality, this is not the case at all. There are millions of addicts who have never used mood-altering chemicals in their rituals of getting high. There are hundreds of thousands of food addicts, addictive gamblers, sex addicts, shoplifters, workaholics, addictive spenders, and many others who are living lives of emotional isolation, shame, and despair caused by their own brands of addiction. This book is written for them and their struggle to have their suffering understood and their addictions recognized. It is also written for addicted people to help them better monitor their identified addictions and prevent their transformation into other addictions.

PART ONE

ADDICTION AS A PROCESS

There have been, over the years, many different ways of describing addiction. To cite a few examples, addiction has been described as a moral weakness, a lack of willpower, an inability to face the world, a physical sickness, and a spiritual illness. If you are a family member or a friend of a practicing addict, you may have more colorful ways of describing what addiction is. Nearly all descriptions have elements of truth about the nature of addiction.

In the next few pages, I'll present a description and definition of what I believe addiction is. Let's start with a basic assumption about most people: nearly all human beings have a deep desire to feel happy and to find peace of mind and soul. At times in our lives, most all of us find this wholeness of peace and beauty, but then it's as if it slips away and is gone, only to return at another time. When it leaves us, we feel a slight sense of sadness and even a slight sense of mourning. In many ways, this is one of the natural cycles of life. It's not a cycle we can control.

There are things we can do to help these cycles along, but for the most part they're uncontrollable in the sense that all of us must go through them. We can either accept these cycles and learn from them or fight them and try to be happy all the time.

Addiction can be viewed as an attempt to control these uncontrollable cycles. When addicts engage in a particular object or event to produce a desired mood change, they emotionally believe they can control these cycles. And at first they can. Addiction, on its most basic level, is an attempt to control and fulfill this desire.

Addiction must be viewed as a process that is progressive. Addiction must be seen as an illness that undergoes continuous development from a definite, though often unclear, beginning toward an end point.

We can draw a strong comparison between addiction and cancer. For us to understand all the different forms of cancer, it is beneficial to understand what all these different forms have in common. What all cancers share is a similar process — the uncontrolled multiplying of cells. We must therefore understand what all addictions and the process of all addictions have in common: the out of control and aimless searching for wholeness, happiness, and peace through a relationship with an object or event.

I use the phrase "an object or event" throughout this book in referring to an addict who engages in the addictive process. Although there are many kinds of addictions, no matter what the addiction is, every addict engages in a relationship with an object or event in order to produce a desired mood change.

- The alcoholic experiences a mood change having drinks at the neighborhood saloon.
- The food addict experiences a mood change bingeing or starving.
- The addictive gambler experiences a mood change placing bets on football games and then watching the action on television.
- The shoplifter experiences a mood change stealing clothing from a department store.
- The sex addict experiences a mood change browsing in a pornographic bookstore.
- The addictive spender experiences a mood change going on a shopping spree.

- The workaholic experiences a mood change staying at work to accomplish another task even though he or she is needed at home.

Although all of the objects or events I've described are different in many ways, they have in common the fact that they produce desired mood changes in the addicts who engage in them.

Extending the Addiction Field

Addiction has been viewed in a very limited way. The reason for this limited focus is because the treatment of addiction is a very young field. The development of treating addiction on any sizable scale started with the beginning of Alcoholics Anonymous in 1935, which concerned itself with a specific form of addiction — alcoholism. In contrast, most other fields of study start with a general knowledge of the subject and, as time goes on, the focus becomes more and more specific.

Our knowledge about addiction started with a specific form of addiction and is now starting to be transferred to help people with other forms of addiction. Moreover, the addiction treatment field was not started by a group of professionals, but by people who suffered from one specific form of addiction. As more and more about the nature of addiction was learned from these pioneers, it was found that their principles of recovery were also useful to help people with other addictions. As more knowledge was shared, persons with other forms of addictions started using these principles to recover. Thus came the start of Gamblers Anonymous, Narcotics Anonymous, Overeaters Anonymous, Sex Addicts Anonymous, Shoplifters Anonymous, Spenders Anonymous, and other Twelve Step self-help groups.

Presently, our field is learning again. We are starting to ask new questions and are finding answers.

Why do certain principles of recovery work so effectively for all of these seemingly different groups? The apparent reason is that the same illness is being treated: addiction. We are starting to see that there are many forms of addiction; though they are different, they are more similar than dissimilar. This book is about their similarity.

Acting Out

Let's briefly describe what is meant by "acting out," since it's a term to be used frequently throughout this book. Acting out is when an addict engages in addictive behaviors or addictive mental obsessions. Here are some examples:

- Sex addicts cruising a section of town where they are most likely to find prostitutes.
- Addictive gamblers studying a racing form.
- Addictive overeaters thinking about going to different stores to buy food, believing clerks are starting to think badly of them.
- Addictive spenders making a latest purchase.

For the addict, acting out is a way to create certain feelings that cause an emotional and mental shift within the person. It is this shift that the addict desires. By acting out either through thoughts or actual behavior, the addict learns to create feelings of being relaxed, excited, or in control. The addict can also create feelings of fear, self-disgust, shame, and self-hate. Most of all, the addict achieves an illusion of being in control through acting out.

Addiction becomes an attempt to make emotional sense out of life. Addicts emotionally believe they are being fulfilled. The high created by the addictive acting out is often described by addicts as a time in which they feel alive and complete. This is especially true in the earlier stages of the addiction process.

Addictive acting out is a way to escape from the pressures and stress of everyday life, and at times even from the shame and pain created by the addictive process.

Addiction and the mood change created by acting out is a very seductive process. The addict is seduced emotionally into believing that one can be nurtured by objects or events.

We can get temporary relief from objects and events, but we can't get real nurturing from them. All of us have to deal with issues, pains, frustrations, and memories we would rather not have to face. At times, we have all used objects or events to avoid facing certain things. The difference between this and addiction is that addiction is a lifestyle in which the person loses control and gets locked into an emotional evading of life.

Addicts keep delaying life issues as a way of nurturing themselves. All of us have this potential to form addictive relationships with a number of different objects or events, especially during stressful times when we would welcome a promise of relief and comfort.

Because addicts try to nurture themselves through avoiding reality and responsibility, addiction is an ineffective way of self-nurturing. The mood change created by the acting out creates only an illusion of being nurtured.

- The food addict binges after a fight with his partner and finds the illusion of peace. For the moment, he feels full instead of empty, but only for a while. During such moments, there is an intense sense of comfort.
- The addictive gambler gets lost in the action and feels excited, confident, and sure of herself. This time she knows she has picked a winner.

Slowly, addicts start to depend on the addictive process for a sense of nurturing and to define who they are. Their lives become the pursuit of their addiction.

Emotional Logic

Addiction starts out as an emotional illusion. This illusion will be entrenched in the addict before others around the addict or even the addict realizes that an addictive relationship has been formed. The addict starts to build a defense system to protect the addictive belief system against attacks from others, but only after the addiction is well established on an emotional level. On a thinking, intellectual level, the addict knows that an object can't bring emotional fulfillment. Alcoholics have heard the old saying, "You can't escape into a bottle." Workaholics know "there's more to life than just work." Addictive spenders understand "money can't buy you happiness."

The illness of addiction begins very deep within the person. The suffering that is happening to the person is taking place on an emotional level. Intimacy, positive or negative, is an emotional experience. This sense of intimacy is experienced, but not logically thought out. Addiction is an emotional relationship with an object or event, and addicts are trying to get their needs for intimacy met through this relationship. When looked at in this way, the logic of addiction starts to become clear.

- When addictive overeaters feel sad, they eat to feel better.
- When alcoholics start to feel out of control with anger, they have a couple of drinks to get back in control.

Addiction is very logical and does follow a logical progression, but this progression is totally based on what I call *emotional logic*, not thinking logic. A person who tries to understand addiction using thinking logic will become frustrated and manipulated by the addict. This is partly why talk therapy (talking one-on-one with a counselor) is so ineffective in convincing addicts to end their destructive, addictive relationships.

We can sum up emotional logic in the phrase, "I want what I want and I want it now." Emotional needs often feel very urgent and compulsive. Emotional logic works to satisfy this urgency even if it is not in the best interest of the person. Here's an example:

- The addictive gambler tells himself he is done gambling for the week. He has a rough day at work. He feels uneasy so he looks over his racing form to try and ease his feelings, still telling himself he won't gamble anymore this week. While reviewing the racing form, his emotional logic starts to tell him he has found a sure bet. "Why didn't I see this before?" he says. "It'd be crazy for me to miss this opportunity!" Thus, he becomes pitted against himself — one side believing in his "sure thing," the other reminding him of his promise not to gamble. Inside, the emotional pressure builds. Because addiction means getting emotional needs met and relieving emotional pressures, he finally must give in to his urge, especially after he has convinced himself he would be stupid not to grab this opportunity.

Emotional logic pits the person against him- or herself. Emotional logic can be very cunning. In the book *Alcoholics Anonymous*, there is a sentence that reads, "Remember that we deal with alcohol — cunning, baffling, powerful!" I believe this is one of the most truthful ways to describe the emotional logic found in all addictions: cunning, baffling, powerful.

Addiction is More Than a Relationship of Convenience

Normally, people's relationships with objects or events are "relationships of convenience." This means we manipulate objects for our own convenience. These relationships with objects are to make our lives easier and more comfortable. Most people have relationships of convenience with the same objects to which addicts get addicted. Normally, these are relationships where there is no emotional bonding or illusion of intimacy. To addicts, however, the object or event starts to become more and more important as they try to get their emotional and intimacy needs met through this relationship, and it eventually becomes their *primary* emotional relationship. Because they experience a mood change, they start to believe their emotional needs have been met. This is an illusion.

Relationships with objects are, realistically, relationships of convenience. Once a person starts to look to an object or event for emotional stability, he or she is building the foundation of an addictive relationship with it.

At this point, I want to state my definition of addiction, which is a variation of one developed in the chemical dependency field. My definition of addiction is as follows:

Addiction is a pathological love and trust relationship with an object or event.

Addiction is a "pathological relationship." What does this mean? To be pathological is to deviate from a healthy or normal condition. When someone is described as being ill, we mean that this person has moved away from what is considered "normal." The word "pathological," therefore, means "abnormal." Consequently, addiction is an abnormal relationship with an object or event. All objects have a normal, socially acceptable function. Food is to nourish; gambling is for fun and excitement; drugs are to help overcome illness. These are examples of the normal, acceptable functions of these objects or events. Anyone using these objects or events in the socially acceptable way would be seen as having a normal, healthy relationship with them. In an addiction, the addict departs from the normal and socially acceptable function of the object and sets up a pathological or abnormal relationship. The food, gambling, or drugs take on a new function: the addict develops a relationship with an object, hoping to get his or her needs met. This is the insanity of addiction, for people normally get emotional and intimacy needs met through intimate connections with other people, themselves, their community, and with a spiritual power greater than themselves. It is through a balanced combination of these relationships that people get healthy emotional nurturance.

Addiction is Not Reaching Out

These normal ways of achieving intimacy involve reaching out to life. We nurture ourselves by reaching out to others and then in, to ourselves. In addiction, this reaching motion is almost totally inward to the point of withdrawing. Addiction exists within the person. When addicts connect with their addictions, they withdraw.

Whenever addicts become preoccupied or act in addictive ways, this forces them to withdraw, to isolate themselves from others. The longer an addictive illness progresses, the less a person feels the ability to have meaningful relationships with others.

Addiction makes life very lonely and isolated, which creates more of a need for the addict to act out. When the addict hurts, he or she will reach for the addiction. When pain creates an emotional need, the addict turns to the addiction for relief, just as someone else may turn to a spouse, a best friend, or spiritual beliefs for relief.

For the addict, the mood change gives the illusion that a need has been met.

How Addicts Treat Themselves and Others

Because addiction is an illness in which the addict's primary relationship is with objects or events and not with people, certain changes will occur.

Objects are manipulated for our own pleasure, to make life easier; addicts slowly transfer this style of relating to objects to the way they interact with people. For the practicing addict, people become one-dimensional objects to manipulate. As time goes on, it becomes second nature for the addict to treat people as objects.

- The sex addict sees people as sexual objects first, and as people second. People around the addict get tired, frustrated, angry, and eventually fed up with being treated as objects.

Treating people as objects eventually leads to greater distance and more isolation from others.

Addicts treat themselves as they treat others. In treating themselves as objects, addicts subject their emotions, mind, spirit, and body to many different dangers. A lot of addicts live on dangerously high levels of stress. As they continue to treat themselves as objects, this often leads to some form of breakdown.

Objects Are Predictable

Through their relationship with an object or event, addicts begin to trust the addictive mood change caused by addiction because it's consistent and predictable. This is the seductive part of addiction.

- If you are a drug addict and you take a drug, you'll experience a predictable mood change.
- If you are addicted to gambling and you start to gamble, you'll experience a predictable mood change.
- If you are an addictive overeater, you'll experience a predictable mood change when you overeat.

The same goes for sex addicts, workaholics, addictive spenders, and people suffering from any other type of addiction — addiction causes them to experience a predictable mood change.

Because addiction for addicts is predictable, this makes it capable of being trusted. One definition of trustable is, "a person or thing that can be relied upon." Addicts rely upon a mood change and the mood change comes through for them.

People, on the other hand, may not always come through.

- You may be in need of emotional support, so you go to your best friend only to find him or her in greater need of emotional support than you.

In this crazy way, for addicts, objects are more dependable than people.

If you were raised in an addictive or abusive family, you may have learned not to trust people. This will make you susceptible to the seductive illusion of comfort created by the predictable mood change in addiction.

Misplaced Priorities

Practicing addicts want to be first and demand to come first. Their wants become all-important. Objects have no wants or needs; thus, in a relationship with an object the addict can always come first. This quality is very attractive to the addict, and also fits well into the belief system created by emotional logic. Remember, practicing addicts don't trust people. An addict trusts addiction. To trust in people is a threat to the addictive process. For the practicing addict, it's object first, people second.

All of us want fulfillment and are looking for relationships that will give us this. Addiction is a relationship problem; it is a destructive, but committed relationship.

- Two people are involved in a destructive relationship. To others around them, this relationship makes no logical sense. But the relationship goes on for years.

Addiction can be described the same way, except the addict is having a destructive relationship with an object or event, not with a person.

In its beginning stages, addiction is an attempt to emotionally fulfill oneself. In many ways, addiction is a normal process gone awry. Most friendships begin with emotional attachment; friendship is based on getting emotional needs fulfilled. Addiction is a pathological way of trying to reach this fulfillment.

- An addictive gambler is not chasing the win, though this is what he tells himself. What the addict trusts and depends on is the false promise and false sense of fulfillment produced by the preoccupation with gambling and the predictable mood change.

When Addictive Relationships Are Formed

There are times when all of us are susceptible to forming addictive relationships, such as after a loss of some kind. There is pain involved in a loss and the need to replace the lost relationship. A good example is retirement. Studies show that this is a dangerous time for many, when the loss of the work relationship can often be replaced by an addictive relationship. People get older and friends pass away; long-standing relationships start to change; thus, many elderly people form addictive relationships with, for example, television or alcohol and other drugs. They come to trust in these objects, knowing they will be there tomorrow.

The following is a list of times when a person may be susceptible to forming an addictive relationship:

- Loss of a loved one (the closer the relationship the more likely the change).
- Loss of status.
- Loss of ideals, dreams.
- Loss of friendships.
- New social challenges or social isolation (for example, moving to a new community).
- Leaving your family.

Seductiveness in Addiction

What makes the addictive relationship so attractive is the mood change it produces. It works every time, it's guaranteed. No human relationship can make this kind of guarantee. This is where the trust aspect of addiction is meaningful. Addicts trust they will experience a mood change if they perform certain behaviors.

- By gorging himself, the food addict can temporarily control his life and the way he feels.

Thus, through acting out, the addict feels a sense of control. This helps to counteract the total sense of powerlessness and unmanageability the addict is feeling on a deeper, more personal level.

There are many seductive aspects in the addictive process. Addiction is a process of buying into false and empty promises: the promise of relief, the promise of emotional security, the false sense of fulfillment, and the false sense of intimacy with the world.

- The addictive gambler doesn't chase the event (gambling) itself, but what the event emotionally comes to represent: a symbol of fulfillment.

It is not only the relationship with a particular object that is dangerous for addicts — it's dangerous to chase this form of dishonesty. Finding emotional fulfillment through an object or event is an illusion. It's dishonest to believe an object or event can bring anything more than a temporary mood change. Continued dishonesty of this type can produce a new addictive relationship with another object. As all addicts know, objects can easily be replaced — highs come in many forms.

- Addictive gamblers are not chasing the win. If the win was important, gamblers would stop when they won. They are chasing the action, the excitement, the moment, and eventually they chase the losing, for this allows them a reason to chase again.

A friend of mine has a plaque on his wall that speaks well for the seduction of addiction.

Fooling people is serious business,
but when you fool yourself
it becomes fatal.

Intensity Mistaken for Intimacy

Emotionally, addicts get intensity and intimacy mixed up. Acting out is a very intense experience for addicts because it involves going against themselves.

- For food addicts who buy a bag of groceries, eat most of the contents, and then make themselves throw up — this is a very intense experience.
- For sex addicts, entering pornographic bookstores and knowing they'll not leave before having sex with a complete stranger and knowing there's a chance they could be arrested — this is a very intense experience.
- For addictive gamblers, watching a football game and knowing the team they have picked must win by six points so they can make a past due house payment — this is a very intense experience.

While in the process of acting out, addicts may feel very much alive, very excited, very shameful, and very scared. Whatever they are feeling, they feel it intensely. Addicts feel very connected to the moment because of the intensity.

Intensity, however, is not intimacy, though addicts repeatedly get them mixed up. The addict has an intense experience and believes it is a moment of intimacy.

- An alcoholic sees his relationships with "drinking buddies" as deep and very personal, only to have them slip away when the event of drinking doesn't occur.

I've learned a lot about the differences between intensity and intimacy from my fifteen-year-old niece, who is going through a time of life where she mixes up intensity and intimacy. She is "totally in love" with a boy in her class, and is sure they'll marry. She has already decided how many children they'll have and what to name them. It would be an exercise in futility to try and talk her out of her emotional beliefs. All of us around her know she is misled by intensity. What she is feeling is very intense, but not very intimate.

Adolescence is a time of learning the differences between intensity and intimacy. Adolescents make promises of friendship for life; they make extensive plans for the future with friends, only to see them fade over time. Part of the essence of intimacy has to do with time. Intimacy isn't just a moment, but many moments linked together over time. Adolescents usually live for the moment. Practicing addicts are also living for the present moment, using emotional logic. Emotionally, addicts act like adolescents and are often described as adolescent in behavior and attitude. After all, a lot of issues addicts struggle with are the same issues that face adolescents. The difference is that addicts stay trapped in an adolescent stage as long as their illness is in progress.

Objects and Events that Become Addicting

What do different objects and events (eating, gambling, chemicals, and sex) that people can get addicted to have in common? It's their ability to produce a positive and pleasurable mood change. This is where one finds the addictive potential of an object or event.

Both washing dishes and gambling are events, but, for most people, washing dishes produces a much smaller pleasurable mood change. Milk and alcohol are substances, but people don't become addicted to milk because it doesn't have the same mood-changing quality as alcohol. Thus, the ability to produce a positive, pleasurable mood change is needed for an object or event to have an addictive potential.

Availability of an object helps determine whether people will choose that form of addiction. Gambling is outlawed in many states; thus, in those states, fewer people will form addictive relationships to this activity.

The more available addictive objects or events are, the greater will be the number of people who form addictive relationships with them. Food is widely available, and eating is an event to which many people form an addictive relationship.

A person can switch an addictive relationship from object to object and event to event. Switching from object to object helps create the illusion that the "problem has been taken care of," when in reality one dangerous relationship has replaced another. This buys more time for the addict.

- An addict may stop using speed and pot and "just" take up drinking.
- The recovering alcoholic who hasn't accepted his addictive personality may slowly develop an addictive relationship with food, putting on 50 or 60 pounds and remaining as emotionally isolated as when he was drinking.

Addicts need to recognize that at times they will want to interact with the world through their addictions. When faced with stress, addicts may want to reach for an object instead of reaching for people or their own spiritual side.

Once an addictive personality is developed, the active addict or recovering addict will always see the world in a different perspective. Like any other major illness, addiction is an experience that changes people in permanent ways. This is why it's so important that people in recovery attend Twelve Step and other self-help meetings on a regular basis; the addictive logic remains deep inside of them and looks for an opportunity to reassert itself in the same or a different form. Recovering addicts continue to go to meetings and work the program because they continue to be addicts. Recovery is the continued acceptance of addiction and the continuous monitoring of the addictive personality in whatever form it may take.

Addiction must be viewed as a continuum because of its progressive nature. Some people teeter on a thin line between abuse and addiction for a long time; all objects or events that produce a positive, pleasurable mood change can be used and abused as part of an addiction. Addiction is different than periodic or even frequent abuse. This difference will become much more clear in the following pages where I'll discuss the addictive personality: the different changes that occur to addicts, their world, and the people who surround them.

PART TWO

STAGES OF ADDICTION

Before we look at the three stages of addiction, let's discuss the concept of *process*. In this book, I use a process model to define addiction. Process involves movement, development, and change.

Process involves movement in a particular direction. It involves a beginning and possibly an end. Process is a flow, moving from one point to another. Thus, when I discuss addiction as a process, I mean a flow, a movement.

Process can also be viewed as a journey that has a beginning and moves with direction. This direction may not always be totally clear, but it's there.

Process is a set of experiences that indicate a particular change.

Addiction is a set of experiences that indicate a specific movement in a specific direction, bringing a series of changes that take place within a person. It is through the commonalities of these experiences and changes that we are able to describe addiction.

As addiction develops, it becomes a way of life. Rather than being rigid, addiction is continually changing. As it changes, it inflicts changes on the person suffering from the addiction. As we study the stages of addiction, we will be looking at a particular process, a particular journey — the addictive process, the addictive journey.

STAGE ONE: INTERNAL CHANGE

Long before anyone suspects or knows there is a problem, many changes will have taken place deep within the person's personality. Addiction changes people in permanent ways. In Stage One, a personality will be permanently altered. Addiction is so powerful that it has the power to permanently alter a person's personality and the personality of others.

When people enter the addictive process, most will either continue in it for life or will reach a point where they, with the help of others, consciously choose another lifestyle called "recovery." Like many other diseases, addiction grows and develops within, long before it reaches a stage where it is recognized by the addict and others.

How it Begins

The journey starts with the person experiencing the high — the mood change — produced by certain behaviors with objects or events.

- The journey for addictive gamblers starts when they feel a mood change caused by the excitement, the "action" of a first win.
- The journey for compulsive spenders starts when they find their moods can be changed by purchasing something.
- The journey for alcoholics starts when they get intoxicated for the first time and find that an object can make them feel different.
- The journey for anorexics starts when they experience the sense of control brought about by not eating.

All of us, even those who are not addicts, experience similar mood changes; but to the prospective addict, it is new, intense knowledge. In the mood change exists the illusion of control, the illusion of comfort, and the illusion of perfection.

For the addict, these mood change experiences are most often very intense. Research in the areas of alcohol and gambling addictions show that the addictive person's first few experiences are often very enjoyable and very intense; therefore, the intoxication experience is very profound.

- Early on in their experiences, many addictive gamblers have had a "big win" or have been with someone who has had a "big win."
- Many alcoholics can describe in great detail their first drinking experiences long after they had occurred.

For the addict, this intensity gets mistaken for intimacy, self-esteem, social comfort, or any number of things.

Intoxicating experiences bring the knowledge that through a relationship with an object or event, one's feelings can change. People turn toward addiction when they decide they don't like the way they're feeling, and they seek out a mood-changing experience. Not everyone who seeks a mood change becomes an addict. Some people will abuse objects or events for a period of time and then turn to other ways of getting their needs met. Nevertheless, in turning to an object or event for relief, one finds the basic illusion upon which addiction is based: finding relief through objects.

Natural Relationships

There are natural relationships people need to turn to for support, nurturing, guidance, love, and emotional and spiritual growth.

1. *Family and friends.* We get day-to-day intimacy needs met through relationships with family and friends. We develop a better sense of ourselves through feedback from these people. It's also through our relationship with family and friends that we develop a sense of importance to others, and a sense of being needed as we need others. We learn how to help others and how others can help us. We also learn a sense of responsibility, knowing that how we act affects others and

how others act affects us. In our relationships with family and friends, hopefully we learn how to have healthy dependencies.

2. *Spiritual Higher Power.* In spirituality we believe in a power outside of ourselves, greater than ourselves. How spirituality gets defined will vary from person to person. For some, a spiritual Higher Power is a religious God; for others, God is nature or a close, supportive group of friends. Through a relationship with a spiritual Higher Power we learn to perceive and accept a natural order, a natural flow. We learn to see the important space we hold within the world and among other living beings, but we also learn that we're only a piece of humanity. In this way, we learn how to view the world and ourselves with a sense of realism. We also develop a relationship we can turn to when family or friends are not enough or can't be there for some reason. We learn about believing in and about trusting. We learn to have faith, which means we don't have to live only for the moment. We learn to believe and trust there will be future moments of serenity and a sense of well-being.

3. *Self.* Through a caring relationship with ourselves we learn self-nurturing — the ability to love ourselves and see ourselves as one resource we can turn to during times of difficulty. It's through a relationship with ourselves where we learn the most about change, either positive or negative. As we watch and interact with ourselves, we see our vast potential for change. It's through a caring relationship with ourselves that we learn to be caring and patient with others. The relationship we have with ourselves is carried in some form to all our other relationships.

4. *Community.* Through our relationship with the different communities we live in (our home community, our work community, and a recovering community), we learn about responsibility for ourselves and others. We learn to view

relationships within a larger framework: we learn to contribute; we learn to take; we learn to give and receive care from those we have never met; and we learn to be interdependent.

If people do not develop relationships within these four groups, they turn to other types of relationships. This is where addiction comes in. Addiction is a relationship with an object or event that takes place within the person. What all four natural relationships have in common is the fact that people must reach within themselves, but they must also reach out. In natural relationships there is a connecting with others — an act of giving and an act of receiving. In addiction there is only an act of taking. Natural relationships are based on emotionally connecting with others; addiction is based on emotional isolation.

The Addictive Cycle

The true start of any addictive relationship is when the person repeatedly seeks the illusion of relief to avoid unpleasant feelings or situations. This is nurturing through avoidance — an unnatural way of taking care of one's emotional needs. At this point, addicts start to give up natural relationships and the relief they offer. They replace these relationships with the addictive relationship.

Consequently, addicts seek serenity through an object or event. This is the beginning of the addictive cycle. If one were to diagram addiction there would be a downward spiraling motion with many valleys and plateaus.

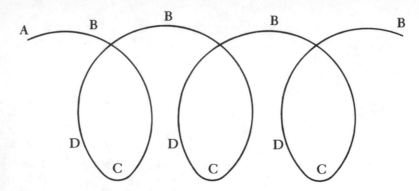

A = pain; B = feel the need to act out; C = act out, start to feel better; D = pain resulting from acting out; B = feel the need to act out; C = act out, start to feel better.

This cycle causes an emotional craving that results in mental preoccupation. For an addict, the feeling of discomfort becomes a signal to act out, not a signal to connect with others or with oneself. The amount of mental obsession is often an indication of the stress in the addict's life. Some addictions produce physical dependency that creates physical symptoms upon withdrawal (as with alcohol and other drugs). Many other types of recovering addicts — sex addicts, addictive gamblers, and addictive spenders — also report physical symptoms when they stop acting out. Whether this is part of the grief process in ending an addictive relationship or actual withdrawal symptoms is unclear — it's probably a combination of both. Addicts who have stopped acting out report feeling edgy and nervous, and these symptoms can last up to a few months.

The Addictive Personality

The most important aspect of Stage One is the emergence of the addictive personality. I believe this is the most important idea expressed in this book. The reason the idea of the addictive personality is so important to understand is that eventually a person forms a dependent relationship with his or her own addictive personality.

Once an addictive personality is established within a person, the specific object or event takes on less importance. When an addictive personality is firmly in control, addicts can (and often do) switch objects of addiction as preferences change or when they get into trouble with one object. Addicts who switch objects of addiction know it's a good way to get people off their backs.

The addictive personality is very important for recovering addicts to understand because the addictive personality will stay with them for life. On some level, this personality will always be searching for an object or some type of event to form an addictive relationship. On some level, this personality will always give the person the illusion that there is an object or event that can nurture them.

The term "dry drunk" describes a person whose life is being controlled by an addictive personality without any drug being present. Dry drunks still trust in the addictive process and cut themselves off from the natural relationships they need in order to be nurtured.

- People in a recovery program for alcohol addiction need to clearly understand that they are prone to form a possible addictive relationship with another object or event — food, for example. For these people, sobriety acquires a new dimension: instead of only monitoring their relationship with alcohol, they also need to learn how to monitor the addictive part of themselves.

I am using the example of alcohol and food here because it's common for a recovering alcoholic to become a food addict. I've met persons who, within three or four years of leaving an alcoholism treatment center, have gained 40 or 50 pounds and are as unhappy and emotionally isolated as they were the day they entered treatment. To quote one such person, "I now find myself eating for all the same reasons I drank: I'm lonely, I'm afraid." Many of these people attend A.A. regularly, are working good recovery programs, and their lives are much better, but something stands in their way of serenity — another addiction.

It's in understanding the addictive personality, even in recovery, that the words, "cunning, baffling, powerful!" show their true meaning. It's the addictive relationship inside oneself that the recovering addict will need to break, not just the relationship with an object. This is when total recovery takes place.

Development of an Addictive Personality

The foundation of the addictive personality is found in all persons. It's found in a normal desire to make it through life with the least amount of pain and the greatest amount of pleasure possible. It's found in our negativism and our mistrust of others and the world, whether our pessimism is big or small, valid or not valid. There is nothing wrong with this part of us; it's natural for all of us to have these beliefs to some degree. It's when these beliefs control one's way of life, as it does in addiction, that people get into trouble. There are persons who are more susceptible to addiction. These are persons who don't know how to have healthy relationships and have been taught not to trust in people. This is mainly because of how they were treated by others while growing up, and they never learned how to connect.

If you were raised in a family where closeness was just a word, not a reality, you are much more prone to form an addictive relationship. This is for two reasons. First, you were taught to distance yourself from people instead of being taught to connect with them. Second, growing up in this type of family left you with a deep, lonely emptiness that you've wanted to have filled. Addiction offers the illusion of fulfillment. If you were raised in a family where people were treated as objects rather than as people, you have already been taught addictive logic. The sad part for many of these people is that many of them struggle hard in recovery; for them, recovery is not a return to a healthier self, but needing to develop a new personality.

Addiction is an active belief in and a commitment of oneself to a negative lifestyle. Addiction begins and grows when a person abandons the natural ways of getting emotional needs met, through connecting with other people, one's community, one's self and spiritual powers greater than oneself. The repeated abandonment of oneself in favor of the addictive high causes the addictive personality to develop and gradually gain power.

The development of an addictive personality is similar to a person who gets up each morning and throughout the day says to himself, "Why bother? Life is hard." The more people tell themselves this, the more they will develop the lifestyle and personality of someone who has given up on life. Every time addicts choose to act out in an addictive way, they are saying to themselves one or more of the following:

- "I don't really need people."
- "I don't have to face anything I don't want to."
- "I'm afraid to face life's and my problems."
- "Objects and events are more important than people."
- "I can do anything I want, whenever I want, no matter who it hurts."

This type of thinking forms a pattern in which a person continually supports and reinforces an addictive belief system found inside oneself. A subtle personality change starts to take place. The fact that in most cases these changes are subtle and gradual over long periods of time adds to the seductiveness of addiction.

Shame

As time goes on and a person continues to act out and is preoccupied and emotionally distant from others, the addictive personality starts to assert more control over the person's internal life. At this stage, the person suffering from addiction will start to feel a "pull" inside. This may come in the form of emotional restlessness or pangs of conscience.

Addiction now starts to produce a byproduct — shame. This happens both consciously and unconsciously to addicts, but mostly on an unconscious level. The more addicts seek relief through addiction, the more shame they'll start to experience and the more they will feel a need to justify the addictive relationship to themselves.

Shame creates a loss of *self*-respect, *self*-esteem, *self*-confidence, *self*-discipline, *self*-determination, *self*-control, *self*-importance, and *self*-love. In the beginning, this shame may be a general uneasiness. It's the first cost an addict pays for the addictive relationship. The person starts to feel shame about the signs of loss of control that are beginning to appear within. There may be an occasional incident of behavioral loss of control, but in Stage One the major forms of loss of control happen on the emotional, thinking level. The person is more apt to feel bad about the internal withdrawal from others. For as the person slowly starts to become more committed to an object or event, there is a gradual emotional withdrawal from intimate relationships with people or a Higher Power.

Where the Addictive Personality Emerges

Addiction starts to create the very thing the person is trying to avoid — pain. In creating pain, the process also creates a need for the continuation of the addictive relationship. *The addict seeks refuge from the pain of addiction by moving further into the addictive process.* The addict seeks happiness and serenity in the high, but because the addict has started to withdraw from oneself and others, the addict can't see that the pain he or she feels is created by acting out.

Long before episodes of being out of control behaviorally appear, the person has fought and lost many battles with his or her Addict on the emotional level, where the addictive personality gains control. An addictive personality starts its development here, at the emotional level. This is the first part of one's personality that becomes controlled by the addictive process.

Addicts act like kids — if it feels good, they do it. They explore; they follow their emotional impulses. Emotions are at the very core of most people's being. This is easily understood when we remember emotions existed long before we had words to describe them or words to help us understand them.

At this stage, the person emotionally feels uneasy, restless, and guilty. These are some of the internal warning signals that one may feel, but part of the addictive process is learning how to deny these warning signals. Addiction is also a process of denial — denial of reality, but mainly denial of the Self. This denial must be accomplished for the addiction to progress.

"Talk therapy" hasn't proven very effective in treating addicts, for the core of the illness exists on an emotional level, not on a thinking level.

How the Addictive Personality Gains Control

Much of an addict's mental obsession results from denial or refusing to recognize the loss of control that is happening on the emotional level. Avoiding the reality of the situation allows the creation of more pain, which will eventually create the need to explain to oneself what is happening. This will evolve into obsessive thoughts or preoccupation and rationalizations. The obsessive thoughts occur more often and consist of constant questioning: *Why?* Preoccupation has to do with acting out and creating a mood change. We've all heard the saying, "Just change your thoughts and you'll feel better." No one knows this better than addicts. If practicing addicts don't like the way they're feeling, they'll think about acting out and a subtle mood change occurs. Each time this happens, the person loses a small piece of control that is transferred to the addiction.

We are starting to see how the gradual loss of the Self occurs in addiction, and how the addictive personality slowly gains more and more control. *The decrease in the Self causes an increase in the addictive personality.*

In addiction, there is an almost constant internal conflict between the Self and the Addict. In this struggle, the Addict wins. This is what is meant by "loss of control." The longer the struggle, the more control the addictive personality gains and establishes. Each time the Self struggles against the addiction, the Addict becomes stronger. To fight and struggle against something that has more power than you drains your energy. For each defeat there is some loss of self-esteem. This is why in recovery people are taught to surrender. It is through accepting that one can't conquer his disease that the person finds strength to start connecting with others.

Everybody has a dream. It may be as simple as having good friends, family, and a peaceful life. Every Addict also has a dream. Advertising contains perfect examples of the Addict's dreams:

- An ice cream store's "mountains of chocolate and rivers of fudge."
- Scenes where all drink happily and no one complains or feels guilty.

The Self also has its own dream. In addiction, the Addict's dream clashes with the Self's dream, which slowly starts taking second place. This is because of the loss of control.

- The intimate relationship a person was hoping to have with a friend starts to be replaced by rivers of chocolate or by alcohol. Addicts find themselves acting and saying things in ways that distance them from the people they love.

The Self and the Addict fight for control in the addictive relationship. As Stage One continues:

- The Addict develops its own way of feeling.
- The Self disapproves of the Addict's beliefs, but enjoys the mood change.
- The Addict develops its own way of thinking.
- The Self fights and argues with the Addict, but loses.
- The Addict develops its own way of behaving.
- The Self makes promises to control the Addict, uses willpower to control the Addict, then works to contain the Addict, but eventually becomes dependent on the Addict's personality.

The addictive relationship is an internal relationship based on the interaction between the Self and the Addict; it is a one-to-one relationship; it is based on emotional logic; it creates an inward focus and isolation; it is sustained by the mood change produced by acting out in the addictive process. The longer the interaction between the Self and the Addict, the stronger the addictive personality becomes; the longer the interaction, the more developed the addictive relationship within becomes. In addiction, the Addict becomes the dominant personality.

People and family members often desperately ask themselves and others, "Why does he act like this? Doesn't he care about us anymore?" The truth is that the Addict within doesn't care about them. What it cares about is acting out, getting the mood change. The Addict doesn't care about the Self either. A statement such as, "At least if you won't stop for me, stop for yourself!" fall on deaf ears. The person who suffers from an addiction often asks the same question long before anyone else: "Why do I act this way? Don't I care?"

I've seen many families gather together in tears, realizing it's the Addict, the illness, the addiction they all hate and fear, not the person. It's often a great relief for people suffering from an addiction to realize that they are not "bad people" as they believed, that their addictive personality is not all of them, but only a part of them, having grown as a result of the illness.

The Illusion of Control

We have seen that over time an addictive personality develops its own way of feeling, thinking, and behaving. When people act out they get high, they feel different, and this changes their thought patterns. Any feeling that creates discomfort becomes a signal to act out; internal clues of discomfort start to become internal clues to act out.

- When a food addict feels sadness, the addictive side will sense this sadness and interpret it not as a real feeling, but as a clue about food. Thus, the person's feelings become mental obsessions. In Stage One the person repeatedly chooses this pattern of distorted interpretation of real sensations.

People often wonder, "Why does she make that choice?" The answer is that by choosing an addictive interpretation of a feeling, the person gets an illusion of control. Addicts chase control — they believe they will find peace and happiness through total or perfect control. To be human is to be imperfect. It's human to be powerless. To chase the illusion of control is to run from the reality of being human. Addicts try to be perfect instead of trying to be people.

Addicts will make addictive choices when they are feeling either powerless, helpless, or weak. The addictive choice creates a feeling of being in control and closer to perfection, at least for a while. The illusion of control is a very tempting offer. Accepting the reality of one's powerlessness in this world is very difficult to do.

Addictive Logic

At times, the person feels something is wrong, sensing the danger of making the addictive choice. Internally, a person starts to question the pathological relationship that is beginning to form. It is due to this questioning that addictive thinking, or what I call *addictive logic*, starts to develop. Addictive logic gets developed as a person tries to justify the subtle changes that are starting to take place within. The first person to experience personal change is the person to whom it is happening. The person may be the last to acknowledge the change but the first to experience it.

It's through the development of addictive logic that the person finds a way to cope with the changes within.

- The food addict starts to question internal urges to eat more often. In the very beginning these urges are simply and quickly dismissed. As their frequency increases, the person starts to explain them away using addictive logic. "It's just something I like to do while watching television." "I only eat like this occasionally." "I'd better get my fill since I'll start my diet tomorrow."

Addictive logic is not based on truth, but totally on the continuation of the delusional addictive relationship. Addictive logic denies the presence of an addictive relationship. The person comes to believe that the problem exists elsewhere or is too big to overcome.

- If addictive gamblers see themselves as having marriage problems, not gambling problems, the addictive relationship will continue.
- If food addicts believe they have no control over what they put in their mouths, they are helpless to do anything about it.

Some may ask:
"Why do they eat themselves into loneliness?"
"How could they gamble away their homes?"
"How could they drink away their livers?"
"How could they have sex with total strangers who may hurt them?"
"How can they take a drug not even knowing what it is?"
The answer to these questions is simple through an understanding of addictive logic. Most people, and even those who suffer from addiction, try to understand addiction and make sense of addictive behavior by using normal logic. This does not work.

Normal logic tells us it's not right to hurt one's Self; addictive logic says it is all right to hurt one's Self because the Self is not important; it's the mood change that counts.

Normal logic tells us it's not right to hurt others; addictive logic says it is all right to hurt others because relationships with people are not important. What is important is a relationship with an object or event.

By looking at addictive logic, we start to see and understand a person's addictive personality.

When an alcoholic says, "I truly don't care what you think of my drinking," one gets a sense of an addict's view of relationships.

When the addict says, "I'm not hurting anyone but myself," one gets a true glimmer of the addict's feelings and beliefs about the Self.

Keep in mind that in Stage One the addictive personality seems less frightening and more of a friend. This forms the basis for what is known as *euphoric recall* — remembering the pleasurable aspects of the addictive process and denying or forgetting the pain. In Stage One, acting out and the mood change create fun, excitement, new ideas, and new stimulation in the person's life. It is not until Stage Two that the acting out starts to lose some of its seductiveness. The object or event always retains its ability to change one's mood, but over time much of the fun starts to vanish and the acting out takes on a maintenance quality — the person acts out more and more to cover up and escape from the pain and frustration created by the addiction process.

The Addictive Delusional System

Slowly over time, addictive logic develops into a belief system — a delusional system from which the person's life will be directed. The person will fight this and delay it as long as possible, but eventually the delusional system and the addictive personality takes over control.

As the illness progresses, the delusional system will become more complex and have a quality of rigidity. The delusional system is commonly described as a wall surrounding the person. This wall has two main functions. First, it serves to keep one locked inside oneself with only the Addict inside to relate to. An addict's world is a lonely one; an addict's focus and energies are directed inward. If a person tries to break from the addictive world, he or she is confronted with the addictive delusional system.

- An addict asks himself, "When is this going to stop?" He hears an idle promise or a voice within saying, "It's not that bad."

The second function of the delusional system is to keep away people who would endanger the addictive relationship.

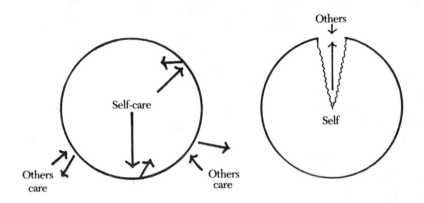

Studies show that during a crisis there is often a crack in the delusional system, and this is a time when the addict's Self and concerned others can connect with the addicted person and provide help. Within a day or two, however, this crack will repair itself and everything will return to normal, often with the person not being able to remember what had happened.

When Recovery Takes Place

By accepting and taking responsibility for the presence of an addictive personality, addicts can start recovery and choosing relationships that allow them to move outside of themselves. True acceptance of the presence and strength of an addictive personality forces addicts to seek help outside of themselves.

The first step in recovery is the acceptance of the dual personalities created in addiction. By accepting the two sides of their addiction, people often create a door that opens outward, allowing them to establish healthy relationships. This frees them from shame. In recovery, the person will need to take total responsibility for both the Self and the Addict. Denial of an addictive personality is part of a practicing addict's life. Thus, admitting the presence of an addictive personality is the basis for recovery.

By acknowledging and claiming the addictive personality and then coming to understand and listen for addictive logic, the person enters into a quality recovery. Programs of recovery stress being totally honest with one's Self. This means listening to and believing in one's Self and not one's Addict.

Before going on to describe Stage Two, I want to quote a short phrase from Robert Louis Stevenson's *Dr. Jekyll and Mr. Hyde,* a title that people often use to describe the personality change from Self to Addict. The book contains much knowledge about this personality change and is a beautiful metaphor about the addictive process. In one section of the book, Dr. Jekyll describes the loss of his Self.

> . . . whereas in the beginning the difficulty had been to throw off the body of Jekyll, it had of late gradually but decidedly transferred itself to the other side . . . I was slowly losing hold of my original and better self and becoming slowly incorporated with my second and worse self. . . .

STAGE TWO: LIFESTYLE CHANGE

Once an addictive personality is firmly in place, the behavioral aspects of addiction become more prevalent. The most publicized aspect of addiction has always been the behavior of addicts, which is the most observable part of addiction and thus the easiest to focus attention on. Addictive behavior — such as addictively overspending, going to pornographic bookstores, and bingeing and purging on food — regularly occurs only after the development of an addictive personality. These behaviors are all signs that the person is out of control on an internal level. In Stage Two, the person also becomes out of control on a behavioral level.

In Stage One, the person was able to contain addiction to the degree that there may have been few episodes of being behaviorally out of control. In Stage Two, these episodes become more and more frequent; the person becomes much more preoccupied with the object or event. It is in this stage that others start to notice that something is wrong, something is not normal. Others start to sense and see the presence of an addictive personality.

In Stage One, the person behaved mainly within socially acceptable limits. The addictive gambler gambled mostly within acceptable limits; the food addict ate mostly within normal limits; the alcoholic drank socially most of the time. But all of these people, internally, started to develop a deep and totally consuming mental dependency.

In Stage Two, a *behavioral dependency* starts to develop. A behavioral dependency is when a person starts to act out the addictive belief system in a ritualistic manner, and the person's behavior becomes more and more out of control. Once an addictive personality has established control emotionally and mentally, the person becomes dependent on the addictive personality, not on the mood change or the object or event. The addictive belief system becomes a person's foundation, and it develops into a lifestyle.

It is in this stage that addicts start to arrange their lives and relationships using addictive logic to guide them. In Stage Two, the behavioral commitment to the addictive process has become all-encompassing.

The Addict's Behavior

There are many ways a person's behavior becomes committed to the addictive process, bringing about an addictive lifestyle.

- The person starts to lie to others, even when it is easier to tell the truth.
- The person starts to blame others, knowing others are not to blame.
- The person starts to ritualize his or her behavior.
- The person starts to withdraw from others.

Not only emotionally and mentally will the person have a secret world to withdraw to, but most often the person will literally have a secret world where he or she retreats to an addictive lifestyle.

- It is in this stage that food addicts may start hiding food or starving themselves.
- It is in this stage that sex addicts may start going to prostitutes, or having multiple affairs.
- It is in this stage that addictive gamblers may open secret bank accounts or get secret jobs.
- It is in this stage that alcoholics may begin to have a couple of quick shots and a few breath mints before going home.

Each of these examples shows a behavioral commitment to the addictive process. Each time people act out in these ways, they are depending more and more on the addictive personality and its logic and less and less on themselves and others who love them.

Addicts must make sense of this to themselves, and they must be able to deny the fear and pain caused by their inappropriate behavior. This is where the addict turns to denial, repression, lies, rationalizations, and other defenses to help cope with what is happening.

Thus, whenever addicts act out and then explain it away, they unintentionally deepen their commitment to addiction. Whenever addicts act out, they must emotionally and mentally withdraw into the addictive personality to receive support for acting out. This inward motion causes them to become more isolated and withdrawn from the world and others around them. They lose more of their humanity. This creates loneliness and a longing to reach out and connect, which internally becomes another signal to act out.

The addictive process has the power and ability to create a need for itself. Through repeated acting out combined with the mental obsession, another form of commitment to the addictive personality will now steadily establish more and more control. The behavioral loss of control is an expression of the internal loss of control by the Self to the Addict.

EXAMPLES OF ADDICTIVE PROMISES

<u>Addict</u>: "Bring me your pain, I will give you relief."
<u>Translation</u>: "Bring me your pain, I'll give you the illusion of relief."

<u>Addict</u>: "I will set you free."
<u>Translation</u>: "I will come to own you."

<u>Addict</u>: "Spend time with me, you can trust me, you can't trust anyone else."
<u>Translation</u>: "Spend time with me, I'll teach you to be mistrustful of others."

<u>Addict</u>: "I'll teach you a way in which you won't have to face issues."
<u>Translation</u>: There is no translation here. The statement is a lie.

Addictive Rituals

Rituals are very important to the addictive process. It is in Stage Two that the behavior of the Addict will become more and more ritualized. The reasons the Addict develops rituals are many. Let's look first at the functions rituals serve in general, and then how this is relevant to the addictive process.

Rituals are important to all of us for many reasons. First, rituals help to bind us to our beliefs and values, and connect us to others with similar beliefs and values. We reassure ourselves of our beliefs and values through our use of rituals. Whenever we are involved in a ritual, it will strengthen our ties to whatever it represents.

Erich Fromm states in *Sane Society* that in a ritual a person "acts out with his body what he thinks out with his brain." Rituals are value statements. In addiction, rituals become value statements about the beliefs of the Addict. These rituals can be, and often are, totally opposite from the beliefs of the Self. So, in addiction the person acts out with his or her body the addictive logic existing in the brain.

Rituals are a form of language — a language of behavior. Rituals speak about our faith and about our current beliefs and values, either positive or negative.

- When we go to a family birthday party, rituals help tie us to our family. Many things at the birthday party are predictable: who will arrive on time and who will arrive late; who will make the dumb jokes at the wrong times; and who will make serious conversation. Our involvement in this ritual becomes a statement to everybody (especially to us) about what we believe is important. We also come to believe that the way we act is the right way to act. Even if we don't like going to a family birthday party, after we've gone we believe it was the "right thing" to do.

Part of the way we are to act is prescribed by the ritual itself. The ritual says "act this way," so we act that way. When the ritual is a birthday party, people sing "Happy Birthday," smile, make cute comments to the person whose birthday it is, bring presents, and eat certain foods.

When addicts are involved in addictive rituals and behaviors, they too act in prescribed ways. They are making behavioral statements that support the addictive process and addictive belief system, just like attending a family birthday party is making a behavioral statement in support of one's family and the family's belief system.

Besides binding us to beliefs and values and to others with similar beliefs, rituals tend to bring us comfort because these rituals are predictable. There is a rigidity found in most rituals. Rituals are based on consistency: first you do this, and then you do that. The comfort may not always be noticed, but it is almost always there. It is most often noticed when the sequence of the ritual is changed or part of the sequence is left out, and we notice our discomfort. Addicts ritualize their behavior for the comfort found in predictability. Addicts also ritualize their actions around behaviors they find exciting; they feel comfortable knowing the excitement will be there if they act in certain ways.

Rituals are designed to bring us comfort at times of crisis or during times of conflict. By engaging in ritualized behavior we are brought back to our beliefs and hopefully the comfort that is to be found within them. When our lives are in turmoil, we tend to seek out consistency. When skies look stormy, we try to get back to our home port. Addicts do the same: when they face crisis and stress, they run to the comfort they find in their rituals. For addicts, addictive rites will tie them not only to a belief or value, but also to a mood — a feeling in which they've come to have faith and find comfort.

Thus, rituals are statements about what people have faith in. Addicts no longer put faith in people. The behavioral way in which they turn to an object or event is defined as their addictive rite. This act of turning to an object or event over time becomes a well defined rite. Each part of the rite is important to the Addict and is designed to heighten the mood change.

Addicts also have their rituals of preference. One sex addict I worked with talked about his favorite ritual in great detail. His preoccupation would start on his way home from work. He would stop at a store and buy a pornographic magazine. Arriving home, he would pour himself a drink, and then sit and look slowly through the magazine. After a couple of drinks, and when he reached a certain level of excitement, he would go to his closet and put on his acting out clothes (he had two or three outfits in which he felt quite sexually attractive). He would leave home and go to a topless bar for another couple of drinks. Next, he would cruise certain parts of town looking for prostitutes. He would talk with them, bargaining back and forth, though he would not have sex with them. Then he would go to a porno shop and look through magazines. On his way home, he would stop at his favorite sauna parlor and have sex with one of the prostitutes working there. He would go home feeling shameful and promise himself he would never do this again.

He would act out in this ritualized way two or three times a month. Each part of the ritual was dependent on the part that preceded it. Each part had a certain meaning to him. For example, he would not have sex with the street prostitutes because he saw himself as being above that. In a crazy way, this part of his ritual helped him feel less shameful about his behavior.

Choices and Rituals

It is through our rituals and the faith we have in them that we hope to solve the internal conflict we all feel at times when we are faced with choices. In turning to our rituals, we are making a choice. *Should I do this or should I do that?* When one turns to a ritual it is a statement that a choice has been made. The choice may not help to solve the issue, but a choice has been made. A person with an addiction feels a great tension inside: *Do I act out or don't I act out?* This tension can go on for days or weeks at a time. It can almost be ever-present. A large part of the suffering caused by addiction is the tension. The addictive ritual will ease this tension, for when an addict is involved in a ritual, this conflict is momentarily over: a choice has been made. There is a sense of release.

Addicts may then face a different type of stress or tension, one caused by the shame of acting out. But the internal tension of *do I act out or don't I?* has been solved for the moment. This release of tension is shown in the example given above: a sex addict would internally debate whether or not to act out as he drove home every night. Most often he would make it home safely. But as soon as he made the decision to stop at that first store and buy a porno magazine, then his evening was not his own anymore. His Addict took over. He felt at ease at that moment, for the internal struggle was over. He had surrendered to his addiction. The debate, the battle between Self and Addict, was over. Sometimes he would give in just to shut the voices up. His release of tension helped to reinforce the choosing of the addictive process. Inside, he must have felt at ease for the moment because a course of action had been chosen. There is peace found in surrendering. I call this *negative surrendering.*

The Community and Rituals

The community to which we become tied will give us direction and rules of conduct. The rituals we perform will always tie us to some community, even if we perform the rituals alone. If we say a certain prayer in private, it will help tie us to the group that uses and believes in that prayer.

Addictive rituals most often take place alone or within a group that has no real caring connection to each other. Most often the group's only connection is their common form of acting out.

Addictive relationships are very superficial and are very private. The Addict is given complete control. The Addict inside does not care to be with people, but prefers to be alone or with other addicts who know, accept, and are not scared by their rites of addiction.

- The alcoholic drinks alone or with "drinking buddies."
- The bulimic's rite of bingeing and purging is a private act, but in another way this ritual is still a tie to a community whose members are secret to each other. Perhaps they will only meet when they band together in recovery to help each other fight their common enemy, food addiction.
- The addictive gambler most often prefers to be alone, but can recognize other addicts by the way they act, by the symbols they carry, and the places they meet. They often pass each other, recognizing each other's presence in a silent way; if they talk, it is about their common interest in gambling.
- The sex addict goes to the X-rated movie theater only to be alone in a private, addictive world. If there is acting out with someone, it often takes place without words, but with addictive looks to communicate who will do what in the addictive rite. Each then leaves to walk away in the silence of one's addictive shame.

Addiction is a negative form of worship, an act of worshipping through connecting with one's negative side, the Addict, at the expense of the Self. The Self always witnesses the addictive ritual and is often sickened by what it is forced to watch and participate in, but it is being held captive by the power of the disease.

Commitment and Rituals

The purpose of any ritual is to deepen one's commitment, to move a person deeper into a certain view of the world. Addictive rituals also have this same purpose, pushing a person deeper into the addictive process. Each time a person acts out, the addictive belief and defense system is strengthened. People who suffer from addictions must either turn to addictive systems (using addictive logic) to explain away their actions or else they'd find these actions hard to accept.

Our culture is made up of many groups, and each group has its own rituals which have rules of conduct that will help bind its members together. This is no different for addictive rituals. Knowing and participating in the rituals of a group is a sign of membership within that group. If a person does a certain behavior, then that person is a member of a certain group.

There are often initiation rites into a group. When I was a child, my friends and I formed a secret club. As we were initiated into the club we were taught how to make a certain sign. This sign was to be a way for us to recognize one another (not a hard task, since there were only four of us). As part of initiation, we took a vow which, if broken, had horrible consequences. Whenever we would see each other at any club meeting or on the street, "the sign" was given and we would feel special and included. Our commitment to our club was strengthened. We believed in our club and the friendship for which it stood. As we grew older and our interest in secret clubs started to fade, our use of "the sign" faded away too, but we found other ways to show our friendship.

I'm sure if I were to see any of my three friends today and show them "the sign" there would be smiles, and conversation of old memories would follow. For a moment we would be connected to each other as club members again. Our ritual did have a power, and that power bound us as friends. "The sign" represented our commitment to each other — it was a statement about our relationship and importance to each other.

For addicts, the object of their addiction becomes symbolic of their relationship to the world. It is a statement that, for this time of life, they are choosing relationships with objects or events over people and spiritual relationships. In this way, every time the addict is engaged in an addictive ritual, the object or event takes on more power. As a symbol, the object gains more and more power. Addicts are fanatics about their rituals.

- Food becomes a powerful symbol for the food addict.
- Sex or anything sexual is all-powerful for the sex addict.
- For the alcoholic, the use of alcohol comes to be a part of sacred ritual, more powerful than life itself.

Developing Healthy Rituals

All addicts develop some form of rigid ritualistic acting out. This is important to understand, for recovering people need to accept that their Addict has chosen preferred ways of acting out, and that there are danger areas, times, and behavior they need to avoid.

- If you are a recovering spending addict and Friday evenings were times when you were most likely to act out in your ritualistic ways, you will need to make sure you are around safe friends on Friday nights for some time to come.
- If you are a sex addict and part of your addictive ritual was to cruise a certain part of town, you will need to stay away from that part of town for some time to come.

Healthy rituals bind us to others, to family or friends, to helpful spiritual principles, or to a community based on helping each other. In this sense, *addictive rituals are reverse rituals*: their primary purpose is to isolate one from others. Healthy rituals help us feel better about ourselves; addictive rituals make us feel worse about ourselves. Healthy rituals bind us to people who care for us; addictive rituals bind us to the dangerous side of ourselves or others. Healthy rituals help us have better relationships; addictive rituals destroy relationships. Healthy rituals help us to feel pride about ourselves and friends; addictive rituals cause shame. Healthy rituals are about celebrating life; addictive rituals seek out death.

Inner Struggle

A person suffering from addiction believes he or she should be able to control the addiction; thus, each time the person acts out, the Self feels more shameful. Most often, the Self disapproves of the Addict's belief system and its treatment of others, but due to loss of control, is unable to stop this process. It is in Stage Two where the person starts to sense and eventually surrenders to the immense power of addiction.

In Stage Two, the person tries to establish behavioral limits, but that also doesn't work. This causes more shame within the person. Eventually, the person surrenders to the presence of the addiction.

Before surrender occurs, however, the person starts to work to contain the addiction instead of trying to overcome it. The major part of addiction still takes place internally, and a major portion of the person's energies are directed inward to the addictive relationship. This causes more isolation. A practicing addict is an emotional loner, truly preferring to be alone. The presence of other people — especially someone who wants to be close — is an annoyance. But at the same time, the Self can be craving a human connection — someone who can help, listen, and hear what is happening.

People Problems

As the illness progresses and the person becomes more and more inwardly directed, others surrounding the person will sense this emotional withdrawal and react to it. This will be the start of "people problems" for the addict.

Since an addict's primary emotional attachment is to an object or event and not to people, many changes take place in the addict's life. Addicts start to manipulate people and treat them as objects; it doesn't make much sense to them that others are offended by this. An addictive personality is often very self-righteous and self-centered.

I remember one addict I worked with who lied to his wife about his behavior and went into a rage when she dared to question him. He asked me, "Why should I talk with my spouse if she isn't going to believe me when I say something?" This question would be justifiable in a normal relationship, but addiction is an abnormal relationship.

To an addictive personality, other people's concern is seen as a problem. People are seen as nosy, and their concern becomes an obstacle to be overcome. People are unimportant unless they can be used to deepen the addiction.

Another reason addicts find comfort in having a primary emotional relationship with objects or events instead of people is because objects or events don't ask questions. Objects will never complain about the way someone acts, and objects don't appear to make demands. These aspects of the addictive world become more and more attractive as the illness progresses and the addict's mistrust of others grows.

In this stage, if family or friends try to connect with the person to find out what is happening, they will be met with some form of resistance — often a lie, silent withdrawal, or even an attack on their dignity.

Addicts start to mistrust others because in Stage Two they project their belief systems and addictive values on everyone else. The addictive belief system believes everyone uses everyone else (because people are just objects) and that you must "do unto others before they do unto you." Most persons who suffer from addiction reject this belief, but they have no resources to fight it. It's not the Self who is in control, it's the Addict. This causes them more shame, and they often start to feel victimized, sorry for themselves, and despairing. In feeling victimized, the person looks for someone or something to blame as the villain, and it is usually someone close.

The saddest part of this is that, in reality, it's the addict who is the victim. Like any other illness, addiction is an assault against a person, but the addict never thinks about this in any meaningful way. To see what is happening as the result of addiction could be a threat to acting out. Most often, the anger and stress addicts feel is projected toward others, themselves, and the whole world.

The attacks, the withdrawal, the lying, and the denial are all, at this point, acting-out behaviors. It's through these forms of acting out that internal pain is created, justifying the next binge. Friends, family, and others around the addict continue to try to connect emotionally with the addict's Self. They come up emptyhanded and, at some point, change the relationship with the addict to emotionally protect themselves. To have a relationship with a practicing addict is very painful and emotionally dangerous.

How Others React to the Addict

Friends and especially family want to make sense out of what is happening to someone they deeply care about. In trying to understand, people around the addict "label" the addict in an effort to cope with the changes.

What is really being labeled is the presence of an addictive personality. The addict may get labeled as "irresponsible," "troubled," "tense," "crazy," "strange," or "weak." If people suspect the true source of the problem, the addict will be labeled more accurately to reflect what is happening. You can often hear the labels a family has come up with if you listen to them talk about the addict. Here's a list of some labels families use:

"He's a bum."
"He eats too much."
"She's so irresponsible."
"All he does is buy, buy, buy!"

"All she does is work, work, work!"
"He does drink a little too much."
"He's oversexed."
"You just can't trust him anymore."

When the labeling process occurs, it's a sign that the illness has progressed to the point where family and friends have noticed it and must protect themselves from the addictive personality. People sense the addict doesn't care about others. They will protect themselves by either removing themselves from or trying to control the addict.

Thus, for families, the labeling process is an attempt to control what is happening. Addicts then react and protect themselves. In doing so, the addictive defensive system becomes even better developed.

Becoming Dependent on the Addict

For the addictive process to continue, the addict must learn how to deflect the concern of others. One of the most dangerous aspects of the labeling process is that, once the addict is given a new label, the family starts to adjust to the "new person." Soon, a need for the addict gets established within the family, which becomes dependent on having the addict around. "The Addict" becomes a role within the family and starts to serve a vital purpose. Family members may not like the Addict, but at some point the Addict becomes one of the family. Family members are caught in a dilemma: they hate the Addict but love the Self within the person. It's not typical for family members to realize they're dealing with an illness; as the addiction progresses within the family, everyone slowly adjusts to the illness.

People start to see what a good scapegoat a person suffering from addiction can be. They start to hate the Addict. As a family member feels attacked, used, and abused by the Addict, it becomes easy to want to get even and fight back. In this way, family members start to get locked into the same fight that the Addict and the Self are locked into. Every family member might ask,

"How can I get the addict to act responsibly and treat me respectfully?" The family tries to make this happen, but fails because a practicing addict isn't respectful. Family members feel ashamed and blame themselves (the exact process that is happening to the person with an addiction). As the struggle goes on, everyone tries to fix the situation, but this fails. Everyone feels worse and gives up for a while and starts to feel ashamed. Then it's back to the work of trying to get the practicing addict to understand and act respectful. This ritual becomes embedded within the fabric of the family. Here's an example of a family's dilemma:

- You love a family member who suffers from an addiction and is unable to love you back. You have deep mood swings, as the person you love swings from the Self to the Addict. One minute you may be relating quite well to the person's Self; then something is said that awakens the Addict. The personality shift occurs, and the next minute you are hating the person, trying to figure out what happened. Was it something you said? All you said was how you wished you could spend more time with the person. You meant this as a caring statement. But you didn't realize that the person is feeling very ashamed of having acted out last night instead of being with the family. So the dragon is awakened, and out comes the Addict to protect his or her territory.

Because the person suffering from the addiction acts untrustworthy, we begin not trusting the person. We internally label the person "untrustworthy." When we can't trust someone, we consciously or unconsciously start to distance ourselves. This is a natural way of protecting ourselves — we need to do this. When the person starts to act like his or her Self, not like an Addict, family members start to feel ashamed for having distanced themselves. They decide to try once more, only to feel betrayed once again. This goes on and on until a family member can't take it anymore and gives up trying to have any relationship with the person. But whenever family members feel the person's Self, they will feel a longing to connect, but also a sense of shame for not wanting to.

Increasing the Addictive Process

In the negative label that gets attached during the addictive process, an addictive personality finds more freedom to act irresponsibly. Permission is always part of a negative label. Addicts also negatively label themselves, and this adds much shame to their lives. The labeling process is frightening for both the addict and the family involved, for it is acknowledging the danger they now live with daily. The labeling process is but one change that is happening to the addict and to people surrounding the addict.

Another change that is happening is the completion of the delusional system. It's through the dishonest interaction with others that the delusion system of the addict becomes complete. In Stage Two an addict's delusion system and defense system are used over and over again and are relied upon more and more. The addict begins to feel more confidence in the ability to manipulate others, but the addict's Self feels more shameful, lost, and isolated. Addicts feel like strangers within themselves. No one knows better than those who suffer from addiction the pain, anger, and despair of being emotionally and spiritually cut off from others and from themselves. It's due to the continued discomfort of this emotional and spiritual desperation that the Self reaches to the Addict for relief.

It is the deep fear, anger, hurt, and pain caused by the addictive process that sends addict's running further into their addiction as they search for relief. When I was at a fair, I saw a six-year-old boy trapped in a house of mirrors. He was crying and screaming uncontrollably, frantically running deeper into the maze, attempting to find a way out. Someone had to go into this house of terror to retrieve and comfort him. People suffering from addiction feel much like that small boy.

Pain and anger fuel the addictive process and are major by-products of addiction, both for addicts and those who surround them. As pain or stress increase, the addict feels more justified in acting out. Because of this and because over time addicts adjust to the mood change produced by their acting out, they feel a need to act out more frequently and with greater intensity.

Being Out of Control

Addicts develop what is called a "tolerance," which simply means they get used to the mood change produced by their acting out. Because of this tolerance and the increased anger and pain levels, addicts in Stage Two start to act out more frequently and in more dangerous ways.

- Addictive overeaters who binge more often and feel increasingly worse about it may decide it makes sense to eat as much as they want. They then take a laxative so as to not gain any weight. They feel shameful about being out of control and eat more in an attempt to feel better.

Episodes of being behaviorally out of control are very frightening for addicts because something they have felt inside for a long time is confirmed: they are out of control. These episodes are often followed by a flurry of promises to stop acting out and start "acting right." These promises are made to convince themselves that they are in control or at least will be in the future.

The addict reaches deep inside, gathers all remaining willpower, and "acts right" for as long as possible. But as soon as the fear or shame wears off or gets pushed deep enough inside, the Addict regains full control over the Self, and the person returns to acting out.

At times, acting out can be a way of dealing with the shame. After crazy episodes of acting out, the addict needs to make sense out of it and turns to his or her delusional system and addictive logic for an answer. Using addictive logic, the person finds a way to explain away what is happening. All addictive logic is based on protecting the addictive personality and the acting-out behavior.

- The addictive gambler believes her financial trouble isn't due to gambling, but maybe because of a bad tip, or because her house payment is too big.
- The shoplifter believes his problems stem from his family and his troubled emotions, not from stealing.

Because of the delusional system, it's very hard, if not nearly impossible, for addicts to see the true reasons they are hurting. They believe it's because people don't understand them or because the world is a tough place to live.

Energy Drain

Control, part of the attractiveness of an addictive lifestyle, is believing one has control over one's world. Ironically, it's the addict's search for control that causes him or her to have less of it. Living in a world of objects and events, the increased search for control, the increased loss of control, the increased shame — all lead to more emotional isolation and produce tremendous emotional and psychological stress. Addiction expends a lot of emotional and psychological energy.

To live an addictive lifestyle, addicts in Stage Two rechannel their energies. More energy is redirected to the addictive process. Activities and people who were important in the past are now less important. The person suffering from addiction finds it difficult to live two lives. Thus, something has to go. Time with family, old friends, and hobbies is set aside to make room for the addiction. Energy once directed toward others and the Self in caring ways is now used to sustain an addictive relationship. Addiction will continuously ask for more and because the person is powerless and has lost control, he or she must give in to the demand.

Once again, there is an almost constant battle between Self and Addict. *Should I act out or shouldn't I act out? . . . It's okay to act out! . . . It's not okay to act out! . . . I'll get in trouble! . . . I don't care if I get in trouble!*

This type of conversation goes on and on inside the person. The Self is trying to control the Addict. To stop the battle means to act out. Many people in recovery report having acted out simply to be done with the internal battle of *should I or shouldn't I?* for a brief period of time. This struggle to control the addiction is a huge drain of energy. Like any other progressive illness, addiction will take more of a person's energy, focus, and ability to function, eroding the ability to be a "normal" human being.

Spiritual Emptiness

As the addictive personality gains more control and addicts lose more of their ability to influence their own thoughts and behavior, there is a spiritual deadening. My definition of *spiritual* means being connected in a meaningful way to the world around us. The feeling of belonging and being an important part of the world is lost as addiction progresses. The sense of knowing oneself and one's importance drifts further and further away.

Addiction is very much a spiritual disease. Everybody has the ability to connect with the soul and spirit of others. Because addiction is a direct assault against the Self, it's a direct attack on the spirit or soul of the person suffering from an addiction. A person's spirit produces life; the goal of addiction is spiritual death.

The longer the addiction goes on, the more spiritually isolated the person becomes. This is the saddest and most frightening aspect of addiction. Sunsets, smiles, laughter, support from others, and other things that nourish our spirits come to mean less as acting out becomes more important. Because addiction blocks a person's ability to effectively connect with his or her own spirit, there is little chance to connect with the spirit of others. Relationships with others become more superficial as the illness progresses. Addicts stay isolated or turn to the presence of other addicts who offer companionship and little or no fear of confrontation.

As addiction progresses, spiritual deadening deepens. This may be the most dangerous aspect of addiction. For recovery, there must be a recommitment to the nurturing of one's spirit. The further one moves away from the Self, the harder it is to reestablish a healing relationship. In the beginning of the addictive process, the person grasped the addiction in an attempt to nurture life, spirit, and the Self in the process of chasing perfection. Many recovering addicts firmly grasp the spiritual aspect of recovery because most are extremely grateful to have such a precious gift returned: the Self, a spiritual awareness, and the ability to connect with others in a meaningful, nurturing way.

STAGE THREE: LIFE BREAKDOWN

Stage Three occurs because addiction works so well at producing pain, fear, shame, loneliness, and anger. Addiction creates these feelings in order for the Addict to gain control over the Self. It creates the need for relief, promising that relief will be found in the mood change.

By Stage Three, the addictive personality is in total control. This personality doesn't care what happens to others, nor does it care what happens to the person who suffers from addiction. What it cares about is achieving and maintaining total control over the person and one's environment. What it cares about is getting high from acting out.

I've named Stage Three the Life Breakdown Stage because here the person's life will literally start to break down under the tremendous stress caused by ever-increasing pain, anger, and fear which results from continuously acting out. Addiction is one of the most stress-producing illnesses of all, and people can only take so much stress before their lives and personalities start to break down. There is a point where a person emotionally, mentally, spiritually, and finally physically breaks down under the stress and pain produced by the addiction.

Acting Out Breaks Down

By Stage Three, acting out no longer produces much pleasure. Preoccupation and acting out still produce a mood change, but there is too much pain to escape from. Although the person feels more distance from pain while acting out, the pain's presence is now almost always felt.

The magical aspect of addiction — the intoxication, the high — begins to break down under stress because the person is living on emotional overload. Acting out can start to feel more boring and ritualized. Many recovering addicts report that at this stage their preoccupation with acting out and dwelling in a fantasy world produced as much or more pleasure and relief as acting out did.

By Stage Three, addicts start behaving in ways they never thought possible. The behavior is so extreme that it actually scares the addict. In this stage the dangerous life-threatening aspects of the addictive process become obvious, not only to the addict, but to family and friends. One of the great dangers at this stage is that the addict is totally committed to the addiction process and will not be able to break this cycle without some form of intervention.

Addictive Logic Breaks Down

In Stage Three, addictive logic can also start to break down. The person's behavior often doesn't even make sense to him or her anymore, so the person gives up trying to make sense of it and falls into a lifestyle based entirely on addictive ritual. Thus, addicts cling to a very rigid lifestyle: they start to feel discomfort with anything unfamiliar. Addiction is a very focused lifestyle and rigidity adds a level of comfort to the addict's life. All of us know the peace and security found in familiar rituals and objects — especially in times of stress. The same is true for the addict, who may hate acting out, but finds security in it. It is something the addict is an expert at. Thus, in times of stress, there is a quick retreat to acting out.

New situations become nightmares for the addict. Life is totally controlled by the addictive belief system. Addictive logic becomes very simple at this stage. It's "get high and exist." At this stage, an addict will only deal with people and ideas that add to the addictive lifestyle; anything else is allowed to float by.

Coping Breaks Down

Resolving emotional issues works against the addictive process. The entire addictive process depends on unresolved issues and the stress they produce. Unresolved feelings and issues are excuses to act out at any time. Let's think of a pressure cooker where the safety valve is not allowing enough pressure to release steam. Soon, something has to give. Emotionally, this is happening to the addict. By Stage Three, the addict has so many unresolved feelings that he or she starts to reach a point of great emotional weakness. The person's coping skills do not provide enough safety to deal with the pressures that are being created. Emotionally, the person starts to break down.

The person may cry uncontrollably for the slightest reason. One recovering addict I talked with said she had cried uncontrollably whenever she saw a sunrise. She later realized that she cried each morning because she dreaded the thought of having to spend even one more day living the life of an Addict.

At this point in the addictive process, people may go into fits of rage for seemingly no reason at all. Their anger has piled up and been compacted to the point at which it isn't anger anymore, but rage — at times, uncontrollable rage.

Paranoia results as the addict starts to question everyone and everything. "Why?" becomes a torturous question that's constantly asked inside oneself. This can build into what is commonly called *free-floating anxiety*, which strikes late-stage addicts and can last anywhere from a few moments to days. Those who experience this anxiety feel that the whole world has turned against them and that no one cares about or even likes them anymore. This aspect of the addiction illness can be very maddening for the addict.

Interacting Breaks Down

By now, the fact that an addict's primary emotional attachment is with an object or event, and not with people, has taken its toll. Many addicts start to feel less secure interacting with people, even on a social level. Persons with addictions often start to question their ability to be around others. They start to feel as if people can see right through them.

An addict interacts with others by manipulating and using them to fulfill addictive needs. Doing this takes a certain amount of self-confidence: an ability to assert oneself, or an ability to appear helpless to get others to act as caretakers. In Stage Three, addicts start to feel very unsure of themselves and often start to lose some of their ability to manipulate. They find people to care for them, but these people often do this out of pity or obligation, not manipulation. Many of those who surround the addict recognize the addict's style of manipulation and react less to it or get fed up with it and withdraw. They often have much of their own pain from interacting with the addict and make an emotional decision not to believe in the person anymore. For them, the addict is emotionally dead. In order to protect their feelings, they refuse to see the addict as a person anymore.

By Stage Three addicts are often surrounded only by persons who are staying with them out of a feeling of responsibility or pity, or because they would feel too guilty about leaving, or they're afraid the addict may get hurt if they leave. This becomes emotional blackmail, as addicts also try to promote feelings of pity, fear, and guilt in others to get them to stay around.

The Addict: Wanting to be Alone

In this late stage of addiction, addicts may totally withdraw from others and become true loners. After all, the addict's ritual of acting out is most often a solitary act done with no one around or done only in the presence of other addicts.

- Addictive overeaters most often binge in private.

- The gambling process is a private, internal strategy.
- Shoplifting is a private act.
- Sex addicts retreat into a private world often filled only by other sex addicts, if by anyone.

It's natural that as an addictive personality develops and gains more control in a person's life, relating skills used to maintain personal relationships will start to weaken.

By Stage Three there is little in the person's life that is permanent and doesn't pertain to the addiction. The person has become totally afraid of intimacy and stays away from any sign of it. Addicts frequently believe others are the cause of their problems. They think people can't understand them. Thus, people are to be avoided.

The Self: Not Wanting to be Alone

Deep inside the addicted person, the aloneness and isolation create a center that is craving emotional connection with others. Addicts are afraid of ending up alone. In their desperation, they show a childlike quality: they attempt to connect with others by clinging to family or friends and often become very upset if it appears that people are withdrawing from them.

- When someone leaves the house, the addict has to know where the person is going. The addict will probably ask the person, "When will you be back?" And, "Do you really have to go?"

The person's Self clings to family and friends in this emotionally dependent style.

Addicts behave as if they are telling people to stay away; but when people do withdraw, addicts become quite upset. These phrases can be heard from the addict:

"You can't leave me, you're all I have!"
"Please, please, I'm sorry, I promise I'll do better."
"Oh, just one more chance, I promise I'll straighten up."
"Okay then, leave! No one cares about me anyway."

Addicts panic when family or friends show any anger or pain, even when it isn't related to them. *Is this the episode that will make them leave me?* is the Self's thought. The Addict wants to be alone, but the Self is terribly afraid of being alone. Often at this stage, the only people in the addict's life are family members. This is all right with the Addict, for being with others has always been a burden.

Environmental Problems

Addicts keep testing the boundaries surrounding them. They may have problems with their jobs as addiction begins to interfere with more aspects of their lives. At this stage, addicts are so out of control behaviorally that perhaps they get in trouble with the law. Part of the excitement in acting out may involve breaking laws and seeing just how far one can go. Addicts may need money to support their addiction and turn to illegal activities in order to get it (this is especially true of addictive gambling).

Thus, many addicts may run into financial problems. They spend large amounts of money to support their addiction, and the addiction is threatening their livelihoods.

- Americans spend 4 billion dollars a year on pornography and it might be accurate to say that a good percentage of this amount is spent by sex addicts.
- More than 50 percent of alcohol sold is bought by 10 percent of the people who buy liquor.

Addicts create problems with their environment because their acting out behaviors may far exceed the limits that the culture around them can accept.

- The alcoholic may be arrested for drinking and driving.
- The sex addict may be arrested for visiting prostitutes or asked to leave a job for unacceptable behaviors.
- The shoplifter may be arrested.
- The food addict's family may demand that he seek counseling.

Physical Signs of Breaking Down

The addiction illness may progress to a point where a person develops physical signs of breaking down. Addiction is very stress-producing, and after years and years of emotional and psychological stress, the person starts to develop physical problems. In all forms of addiction, the person's emotional and psychological systems run on overload most of the time. Imagine the stress on the heart and every other organ in the body. Different addictions will, over time, affect different parts of the body — the liver of the alcoholic, the throat of the bulimic, or sexually transmitted diseases from sexual promiscuity. Addicts often don't take very good care of their bodies — it's an object to be used and abused. There isn't any real way to calculate the total physical damage addiction does to addicts, families, and friends.

Thoughts of Suicide

In this stage of the addiction process a person may start to seriously consider, attempt, or even actually commit suicide. There are two reasons for this:

1. The internal pain is so great that the person wants it to stop, but the addictive promise of relief isn't working anymore. Addicts want the pain to stop, but they don't believe they can stop it. An addict doesn't believe in his or her Self anymore. Suicide starts to make sense, especially when using addictive logic.

2. Addicts become so ashamed of and hate the addictive side of themselves so much that they want to end the addictive relationship at all costs — to the point of performing a homicidal act against the Addict. No one hates the Addict more than a person suffering from the addiction.

Stuck in Stage Three

Addicts can't break the addictive process; thus, addicts remain in Stage Three until there is some form of intervention. Those who try to break the addiction process find that addiction is all they know, and they return to the addictive lifestyle. To recover, addicts learn a new lifestyle. They slowly exchange the addictive way of life for a new lifestyle where there are relationships with people. These relationships add to personal satisfaction and allow growth.

The addict's world is based on an inward flow. To recover, the person must learn how to reach outward and sustain this outward flow. For addicts in Stage Three, it's impossible to do this on their own. People with addictions are handicapped because they don't know how to reach outside of themselves. This is why the person will stay in an addictive relationship until there is some form of intervention.

There are many different forms of intervention, which is an attempt to break the addictive relationship. Some are successful, some are not. Like most relationships, addiction can be resumed even if arrested for long periods. How many times have we seen someone end a relationship with another person only to establish an identical type of relationship with someone else? Recovering addicts should keep in mind that addiction is not just a way of interacting with a specific object or event; it's a way of interacting with one's Self and the world. To recover, the person must not only break off the emotional dependency within, but also turn to the Self and others. In doing this, a person can discover a new way of life, which can be wonderful and exciting, though vulnerable to struggles and fear.

PART THREE

SOCIETY AND ADDICTION

Our society has a great influence on who we are and the issues we will struggle with as human beings. Our society holds certain beliefs and values and has come to stand for many things. For example, America has come to stand for freedom and democracy (although high rates of addiction may be stealing freedom and eliminating choice for many Americans). Because our society represents certain values and beliefs, it will also tell us the types of relationships we are to have with others and with the objects that surround us.

All of us live within and are influenced by two major groups, two major cultures: our society and our families. In this section, we will first look at how our society influences and can push its members toward addictions. In Part Four, we'll look at how families can influence their members toward addiction.

How Society Pushes People Toward Addiction

It is important to remember that we are individuals, and as individuals we are responsible for the choices we make. Although our society may have many values that are consistent with addictive values, society also has values that oppose the addictive process. As a society we believe in hope, helping others, and free will. These are examples of some societal values that are opposite the addictive process. We will need to recognize our nonaddictive values and challenge our addictive values if we, as a society, want to become less addictive. Let's now look at values and beliefs our society holds that help to push its members toward addiction.

Looking Out for Number One

Our society is obsessed with being right and looking right. Our society is obsessed with achievement. Our society is obsessed with being "number one." There is always a push to become better, to be the best. Coming in second is okay, but better luck next time. There is a commercial on television where a group of people are waiting for the results of a product test. After the winner is announced, someone asks, "Well, who came in second?" The announcer looks the person in the face and says, "Does it really matter?" Only the blue ribbon seems to count.

I don't believe there is anything wrong with striving and pushing ourselves to become better. My job as a therapist is about this. We have a responsibility to ourselves and others to better ourselves. But the point is that it's not bettering ourselves that society considers most important — it's coming in first that is valued. Being the best is prized above all else. As a society, we attach subtle shame to being anything less than first. The truth that we all live with is that we may not achieve number one. Most of us live in the middle, whether it's playing tennis, or being a mother, father, husband, wife, lover, or friend. Even those who achieve number one in some area of their lives are average in many other areas. There is nothing wrong, bad, or shameful in the fact that most of us are average human beings, but we do not stress this in our society.

The danger with the obsession about being number one is that this is an addictive value. When we are preoccupied with being first we push ourselves and others toward extremes and toward excess; consequently, we push people away from moderation, from their center of balance. In short, we are telling ourselves to live on the edge — not to visit the edge, which can be helpful, but to live there.

Living for Outcomes

As a society, we are obsessed with outcomes. This is another addictive value. Addiction has to do with results and outcomes; addicts are obsessed with outcome. In addiction what is all important is the high, the mood change, whether it is achieved by acting out or by being preoccupied. The addict is outcome-centered. When outcome is all important, what gets overlooked or pushed aside is the *process*. Process is about how one reaches a certain point. If a person overlooks the process, that person is overlooking or pushing aside his or her conscience. Most of us can't overlook our conscience so we learn to deny it. In learning *denial* one is learning how to be an addict. Denial is a key ingredient found in any addiction. In addiction, people have to learn to push aside their conscience at great cost to themselves and others. A person without a conscience is like a ship without a rudder. So, when as a society we tell our members that what is most important is the outcome, we are also teaching them to deny their conscience.

The way we as a society achieve our goals is very important. The way each individual achieves his or her own goals is also very important, for it is in an individual's process of achievement that he or she will find values, beliefs, and spirit. Thus, it is in how we act, not in what we achieve, that will determine if we are happy and have relationships that work for us.

As a society we spend little time discussing process; we want to know what the bottom line is. To an addict, spending time with questions of conscience is a waste of time. What matters is acting out and getting high. It doesn't matter who gets stepped on.

- For addictive gamblers, what is important is placing the bet, getting in on the "action." It's not important if their families are in trouble due to their gambling. "They'll be happy once we've won all the money," the Addict tells the Self in an effort to ease the pangs of conscience.

It is really not a very big jump from "stepping on people to get ahead" to "stepping on people to get a high."

Control

Another addictive value that is also an important societal value is that control is all important. We are expected to be in control at all times. Someone once defined an addict as a person who would rather be in control than be happy. The issue of control, much like our obsession with outcomes, is a thread between society's values and addictive values. Control is also about outcomes, for if you're in control you should be able to control the outcome. Not being in control is seen as bad: a person is often judged as weak, worthless, and not to be respected.

An example of judging a person by the control issue is our society's attitude toward older people and aging. As a society we often see older people as "less than." We see them as not always being on top of things, not always being in control of themselves. We often see them as not having much to offer. We seem to be afraid of older people. As a society we fear getting older and run to our obsession with youth, as if we could protect ourselves from the natural process of growing old. More so than other societies, we tend to abandon people as they go through the process of aging. Many cultures hold their older people in honored positions. They are basically seen as keepers of the process, keepers of how one should do things. They are often seen as teachers of the young. They teach by telling stories, often their own stories — stories with metaphors and morals. In our fast and outcome-centered society older people are often seen as a liability. Their presence seems to slow us down and we don't like this, except perhaps on Sunday or at family picnics. Thus, we tend to make older people disposable.

Older people can be a reminder to us that process is important. Many of them are looking back at their lives and examining not only what they achieved, but also how they lived their lives.

They've watched the world and their bodies age; many have learned that control is an illusion.

Control is at best a percentage. To believe in absolute control is to believe in and chase an illusion. This will create pain within the person and also for those around the person. Pain is a key ingredient in the addictive process. In addiction there is the seductive illusion that a person can be in absolute control. People who suffer from addictions have problems in their lives and feel pain; like anyone else, they want relief. So they act out, experience the mood change and get a sense that they are in control and that their problems are resolved. For the moment an illusion is created that they are in control and things are better. Nothing could be further from the truth. As a society we push the issue of absolute control whenever we tell our members they have to be number one.

Perfection

Another societal value that is also an addictive value is our belief in perfection. We tell ourselves and others to be perfect at any cost. Our obsession with the perfect body is a good example of this. We don't want our bodies to be healthy, we want them to be perfect. From glamour magazines to beauty contests, women's bodies are being judged and expected to be "perfect." Men's bodies are also now starting to be put on the judging block. All the contestants are to be perfect in every way. Everyone is to have the body of a nineteen year old. People cast this societal value off as harmless, but it is not. It is costing lives.

- The anorexic starves to death in search of perfection.
- Bulimia can destroy the insides of its victims.

Who knows how many people have killed themselves because they felt they weren't able to achieve perfection?

Addiction is about chasing the myth of perfection, whether it's chasing the perfect body or chasing the almighty dollar, which is the male counterpart of the perfect body (some may believe all men should be able to make a lot of money).

Perfection is an image, and everyone has a different image of what perfection means. Perfection is a myth we use to beat up ourselves and others. It's a myth because it's unattainable. Although everyone has a different image of what perfection is, everyone is expected to be perfect in the same way. In our society the definition of perfection always seems to be an extreme, an excess. Addicts believe in and push themselves to be perfect.

- The workaholic strives to get to "the top."
- The bulimic strives to have the "perfect" body.
- The anorexic starves to have the "perfect" body.

Most often "the top" is defined by someone else and not from within the person. Striving to be perfect pushes us away from ourselves. It makes us machine-like — a beauty machine or a money machine. When we turn people into objects, we push them away from their humanity. When we see someone as perfect, we stop treating the person as human.

One client I worked with is very beautiful by society's standards. She would talk about what a handicap it is for her to make friends and have people be honest with her. Other females are intimidated by her looks, while males try to make her their prize catch. Few people treat her normally; most treat her as an object.

Humans are not perfect creatures and never will be. If we tell ourselves and others we must strive to be perfect, we are setting ourselves and others up for very stressful, frustrating, and painful lives. We will be pushing ourselves and others away from humanity — where our strength and spirit is to be found. Trying to be perfect creates loneliness, and when we feel alone we are more susceptible to the addictive process.

When we try to be gods, we fail; when we try to be human, we succeed from the very start. We can never become gods, but we can learn to become better people. In *Alcoholics Anonymous* there is a chapter that describes how the program of Alcoholics Anonymous works. Within that chapter there is a phrase that states, "Ours is a program of spiritual progress not perfection." The authors wisely included this phrase to tell people to focus on progress and process, not on outcome. Much pain is caused as people strive to be perfect. The stress of a life dedicated to perfection causes many people to seek the seductive relief found in the addictive process. Perfection is an addictive value; progress is a spiritual value.

Many people walk around beating themselves up and feeling shameful because they are not perfect. A nineteen year old came to see me because he was feeling suicidal. He received two B's on his report card (the rest were A's). Two B's, and he wanted to end his life because he had failed to achieve perfection during one quarter of the school year. He had totally bought the myth that nothing less than perfection is acceptable.

The danger in chasing perfection is what happens to us when we are confronted with the fact that, as humans, we are imperfect. Often, this is a time when we turn to addictive relationships to help us think we can be perfect or to help us deal with the pain of finding out we are only human. We always choose to feel shameful that we failed. We tend not to talk about our failures or disappointments to anyone. The young man I mentioned would be a prime candidate to turn to some object that would promise him relief from his pain and the illusion that he could achieve perfection.

Lack of Genuine Relationships

We live in a fast-paced, temporary society; as a result, there is a lack of emphasis on relationships. In a society where outcomes, not process, are important, people tend to see others as objects. This can cause a mistrust of others. In a society where there is the possibility of reaching the societal goal of "getting rich by suing others," it's not surprising to find people mistrusting and afraid of forming relationships.

Relationships among some people in our society seem to have taken on a disposable quality. People hope relationships will work out, but these relationships are pushed aside if they don't work.

When relationships with people become suspect, relationships with objects or events become much more attractive.

Worshiping Objects

We are encouraged to accumulate as many objects as we can. Status is attached to these objects; thus, you can tell what type of people you are dealing with by the objects surrounding them. It's easier to have relationships with objects than relationships with people. Objects will not put demands on you; objects won't argue or disagree with you. They are there to serve you. The major problem with having a primary relationship with an object is an object isn't very satisfying to get one's emotional and intimacy needs met. People come to feel very alone inside, and believe they need more objects, when what they're craving is human connection.

A Disposable Society

Some of us live our lives believing on some level that our society and the world are just one-half hour away from being destroyed at any given time. A significant number of young people truly believe they will never reach old age because of the possibility of nuclear annihilation. As a society, we live consistently under extreme stress because of this. It is known that some people numb themselves due to the threat of nuclear annihilation. Addiction is about numbing oneself. It's hard to imagine the effect this threat has on us and how it may help to push people toward forming addictive relationships.

There is one major social issue the Soviet Union and the United States have in common: high rates of alcoholism. If we treat our lands, our lives, our children's lives, and other people's lands, their lives, and their children's lives as disposable, we are pushing ourselves and others toward addiction. Addiction is a process in which the addict and those surrounding the addict become disposable. The logic that we become safer by producing more and more weapons is identical to the addictive logic that says it's okay to take more of a chemical that will kill you. This logic treats humanity as if it's disposable.

We have come to see our world as an object to be used, instead of as a planet full of life with which all of us have an intimate relationship. Native American cultures emphasize that we once had a relationship with nature and that this relationship is sacred. These cultures teach that we are part of the earth and the earth is part of us. In this way, we are taught that the most important part of relationships is mutual respect. By following these ideals, it's impossible for anyone to ever be alone. Even when no other person is around, nature is always surrounding us.

If, as a culture, we teach people that relationships are important, we're also teaching people how to monitor their own actions. To have respectful relationships with oneself and others, people have to be able to discipline their own impulses. Addiction works well in our society, for addiction is about trusting in relationships with objects or events, not with people.

What Happens When Things Are Carried to Extremes

Another value our society has that fits well into the rules of addiction is how we value excess. If one is good, then two are better.

- Many drug addicts have said "if one is good, then two are better" as they pop a handful of pills.
- Many food addicts have said this to themselves as their number comes up at the bakery counter.
- Many addictive spenders have said this as they pay for something they know will only end up in their closet.

Excess becomes a status symbol in our society. Addiction is about excess. Addicts love to stock up. From hiding bottles to secret bank accounts, addicts are always trying to get as much as they can. Addicts have a terrible fear of running out. It really is a fear of abandonment. Addicts have abandoned much in their lives — values, friends, and self-respect. Their greatest fear is that their object will abandon them, even though this is impossible. Objects can't abandon people; people abandon objects.

There are many similarities between the addictive process and what our society presently stands for. This may be why the rates of addiction are so high. Nevertheless, as mentioned in the beginning of this section, our society also has values that oppose the addictive process. We seem to be getting fed up with addiction, and are starting to fight against this illness. We are doing so by reclaiming the spiritual aspects of ourselves and hopefully of our society as a whole. A friend of mine once defined addiction as "answering one's spiritual calling by going to the wrong address." Maybe we, as individuals and as a group, are finally starting to show up at the right address.

PART FOUR

FAMILY AND ADDICTION

Often I'm asked, "Do families cause people to become addicts?" My answer is, "I'm not sure." I personally lean more toward the belief that families are not the cause of addiction. We really don't know what causes addiction, although some people will tell you they do know.

What we do know are certain factors and family types that may help to push a person toward addiction. I tend to approach the question of why people become addicts in the following way: I draw a comparison of how one's environment and the level of pollutants found in it can make a person more susceptible to different diseases. If you live in an area with extremely high levels of pollutants in the air and you are vulnerable to respiratory problems (whether it be due to genetic predisposition or other reasons) you will then have a higher chance of developing respiratory problems. Your risk increases the longer you live within a polluted environment. I view family and societal influences in this way. Our society has some attitudes, values, beliefs, and behaviors that can push a person with addictive tendencies toward addiction. Families are the same way. There are certain polluted attitudes, values, beliefs, and behaviors that some families engage in that will push their members toward addiction or codependency. Families have different levels of these polluted attitudes, values, beliefs, and behaviors.

Depending on the levels, family members will have a greater or lesser likelihood of developing the illness we call addiction.

Another example of this is, since both my parents have had cancer, my siblings and I have a higher chance of developing cancer as we grow older. It doesn't mean we'll get cancer, but we have a higher chance of this happening than someone who grew up in a family with no history of cancer. This is very similar for people growing up in addictive families; they have a higher chance of developing an addiction. Is it genetic or learned? At this time we don't know. In all likelihood, it will be found to be a combination of the two.

The purpose of this section is to look at types of families and factors found within families that push their members toward forming addictive relationships with objects or events.

Having Parents Who Suffer Addictions

If you grew up in a family in which one parent was an addict, you have a certain likelihood of developing an addiction. If both your parents were addicts, your chances increase greatly. Families in which there are addictive parents tend to either produce codependents (people who take care of addicts) or to produce addicts. Members of addictive families know and live on extremes.

- Alcoholic families will more likely have children who end up drinking abusively, or children who won't drink at all.

In other words, addictive families produce children who end up on opposite ends of a continuum. It may help if we view a family as a circle. Along comes the illness of addiction and it cuts into the

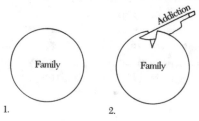

circle. The pain of addiction starts to cause people to separate from one another. This fracture will eventually create both addicts and codependents as family members develop different ways of coping with addiction.

Family members are forced to develop some ways to cope with this intrusion. The addict and the codependent develop internal coping patterns that outwardly appear to be opposite, but are actually very similar. They both have come to be dependent on an illusion. Addicts depend on the illusion that they can escape the pain in their family through an object or event; codependents believe in the illusion that they can stop the pain if they can get an addict to stop acting out.

There is also a danger in that each side eventually becomes dependent on the other. When children from these families are ready to start their own families, they tend to find a counterpart.

- A codependent marries an addict.
- An addict marries a codependent.

Thus, the generational cycle of addiction is formed. The family members have learned the language of addiction; when it's time to form relationships outside of the family, they seek out people who speak the same language. This selective search doesn't take place on a conscious level — it takes place on a much deeper level, the emotional level.

- When I was in Europe and sitting at a cafe having coffee, I overheard some people speaking English. I was immediately drawn to them. They even had an accent that sounded

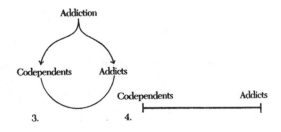

familiar. I could not help but start up a conversation with them. A subtle loneliness that had been inside me was, for that moment, gone. I was again with someone who knew and spoke my language. I felt they knew me and that I knew them. I felt I was with people who understood me, my ways, my values, and attitudes. I didn't want to leave them, for I knew my loneliness would return.

I am often asked by frustrated clients, "Why do I keep connecting up with addicts?" My answer is, "You speak the same language."

By being raised in an addictive family, a person watches and learns addictive beliefs and addictive logic firsthand. This is the language a person is taught; learning in our families takes place as we watch and interact with family members.

If your parents are addicts, they will be teaching you addictive values and logic as you interact with them. They can't teach you about other things. Addicts teach addiction. They may tell you about other things, but their actions will teach you about addiction.

Addictive parents are constantly shifting positions within the family. One minute they may be all-loving, concerned parents, and the next minute they act like an irresponsible child. The child, especially a young child, in an addictive family changes along with the parent in an attempt to stay connected to the parent. Thus, one minute the child in an addictive family will be acting like a child, and the next minute the same child may be acting like a responsible parent. Growing up in an addictive system creates much psychic pain due to these major shifts.

Emotional Instability

Another major shift that occurs is in the emotional level within the family. In the morning everything may be wonderful, but by nightfall a cloud of despair fills the house. Or there may be times when there is too much love, so that it almost suffocates family members, as parents try to make up for their horrible behavior the night before. This constant shifting and lack of stability either on a behavioral or an emotional level leaves family members feeling lost and unsure of themselves.

Children from addictive families often wonder where they stand in comparison to others. They always grow up wanting a normal family. They feel different and develop self-doubt, confusion, and a craving to know what is normal. It is these self-doubts, this confusion and lack of consistency that helps lead children of addicts to develop addictive relationships of their own. They may become addicted to different objects or events than those their addictive parent was addicted to, because they will do anything not to be like that parent.

- The child of an alcoholic may not drink but may instead develop a food addiction.

Consistency helps people feel safe; thus, children need a consistent emotional base from which to develop. The inconsistency in an addictive family makes its members feel unsafe and unsure of themselves. Children feel unsure of themselves and unsure of the world around them since they don't know when the emotional winds may change and the love and caring of the moment will be replaced by put-downs and insults. This creates a sense of dread inside of them. I have worked with a lot of adults who come from addictive families. They speak of a sense of doom that always seems to be following them around. This feeling gets worse inside of them when things are going well. They're sure something bad is going to happen.

- A person believes his relationship with another person is about to fall apart even when there is no evidence to support that.
- A person feels sure she is going to be fired at work even though she was promoted just two months ago.

These feelings of doom come from living in a crisis-centered family, which is what addictive families are. A sense of doom comes from a time when doom was a reality. Good times in an addictive family are not to be trusted. They are followed by crises and personal danger on an emotional level. Family members are in danger until the addiction is dealt with and arrested.

Members of addictive families look for distractions or ways to become numb to the problems. They try to deaden themselves. This is where they may start their own addictive journey.

- Mom and Dad are fighting the same old fight about the debts caused by the gambling. You wish it would stop, but you can't make it end, so you run to the television set, turn it on, and get as lost as you can. Or you run to your room, fantasize, and make promises to yourself that when you get older you'll be rich so no one can hurt you. You've started to share your parents' behaviors. Like your parents, you are trying to numb your pain, or you're chasing a fantasy in an attempt to stop the pain.

Along with these major inconsistencies, a person growing up in an addictive family is taught an insane type of logic — addictive logic.

- You are made to listen as family members try to explain away their behavior as if it were nothing. Inside, you feel crazy as you watch your parents destroying themselves. You tell yourself this is crazy, but then you look around and see other family members acting like what is happening is no big deal.

Family members take turns falling apart, with some members never getting their chance. Inwardly and outwardly, people question the insane behaviors of the addict and other family members. They are met with what pass on the outside as reasonable answers, but in reality are total lies.

- Here you are, being surrounded with insanity, plus you are being taught to lie and say a problem doesn't exist. To lie is to openly deny reality. You ask, "Why is Dad acting angry and yelling at us?" You are told, "Dad just had a bad day at work." The truth is, Daddy is a drunk. Pretty soon some friends may say, "It must be hard for you when your father acts that way." You pass their concern off, telling them how your father doesn't like his job and if he'd get a different job things would be normal.

Children in addictive families, like in almost all families, are taught not to betray the family. But in addictive families, this gets stressed a lot. Many strong messages are given about the importance of family and how all families have their secrets that you don't tell others about. Addictive families have to teach their members to lie — it's part of addiction.

- In being taught to lie, you are pitted against yourself. The healthy part of you knows it's crazy, but as a sign of family membership and loyalty you say it's not so bad.

To survive in an addictive system, children learn to deny their healthy responses that tell them they are in danger; they have to keep increasing these dishonest coping skills because the insanity and the illness keep progressing.

Growing Up in an Abusive Family

All children growing up in an addictive system are growing up in an abusive system. Addiction is a form of child abuse because it handicaps children in their development. The needs of the addict come before the development needs of the child.

I define two categories of abuse: *Intentional abuse* is caused when one person intentionally hurts other people, whether the person regrets it later or not. Intentional abuse can be physical, verbal, emotional, or sexual. *Unintentional abuse* consists of events such as growing up in an addictive family, having a parent who dies early in a child's life, poverty, and other events that happen by random chance. People don't get to choose the family they are born into. In this section we'll be looking mostly at intentional abuse and how it pushes people toward forming addictive relationships.

If you grow up in a family where there is physical, emotional, verbal, or sexual abuse, you are being told that you don't count. Your needs are not important. What is important are the needs of the abusing parent. Your needs as a child — to be protected, to have love and nurturing, to be treated as a human being — get pushed aside. The needs of the abusive parent always come first. You are being taught that you are just an object, an object to be used to fulfill someone else's individual needs. In this way, you are taught the objectification process found in addiction. Addicts treat others as objects, and this is exactly what is happening to the child in an abusive home. It doesn't matter whether the abuse is being directed at you or if you are forced to watch others being abused.

- If you grow up in a family where Father is beating up Mother or in a family where Mother is beating up Father, you are forced to watch people treating others as objects and not as humans. Your humanity is denied. You are taught that people are objects to be used and manipulated for one's own benefit. You are taught people are to be controlled. This will have a major impact on the development of Self within you. You are being taught your Self doesn't count. Over time you'll develop low self-esteem and low self-confidence.

You are also taught by example to have low impulse control. Addiction is an impulse control disorder. As you watch your parents turn to hitting, yelling, or sexually abusing others to handle their emotional distress, you learn how to be undisciplined when it comes to your own emotional impulses. You are taught to be reactive; you go through life not with a sense of consistency, but with a sense of waiting for things to happen to you so you can react to them. You learn not to take initiative but to wait for things to happen.

Growing up in an abusive family also teaches you to mistrust people. Abusive people are dangerous people. They can and do inflict great pain on other people. We develop trust within our families; if you grow up in a family where your biggest danger is at home, where are you to develop trust? Fathers and mothers have an obligation to give their children a safe home environment in which to grow. We all have violent impulses. By watching your parents control or not control these impulses, you are taught how to handle your own violent impulses. Fathers and mothers have an obligation to be as trustworthy and dependable to their children as they possibly can be. If your parents are the two people in the world you should most be able to trust, and they are fighting between themselves and abusing you, then who are you to trust?

To trust or not to trust is a question that gets answered early in our lives, and is learned within our homes. It's part of the language we learn; it's part of the view of the world we are given. Again, the saddest part about growing up in an abusive home is that when the time comes to leave, we usually look for people with the same world view and who speak the same language.

To watch family members destroy the body and soul of one another is excruciatingly painful. Pain is an essential ingredient in the addictive process.

- Here's a young person leaving an abusive home. He has been treated like an object for years. He has been taught to have little impulse control. He's been taught to mistrust people, and he is carrying an enormous amount of psychological pain. He is primed for the types of promises that addiction holds and the relief offered by the mood change.

To me, it is a surprise that not all children from abusive families end up developing addictions.

Growing Up in a Neglectful Family

Neglect is also a form of abuse, but we'll look at it separately because it can be a more subtle form of abuse. Individuals growing up in a neglectful family often don't see themselves as being abused. Growing up in a neglectful family tends to leave people emotionally underdeveloped.

To develop as a child one needs input, interaction, and nurturing. In neglectful families children don't get this. They take up space, but they're never sure if they're special, and never sure if they're important. The Self inside such people becomes underdeveloped. Their self-esteem does not develop to a healthy level. Thus, people leave neglectful homes more susceptible to the seductive element found in the addictive process. Powerful events, powerful people, and powerful objects tend to be seductive elements to them. It is as if these things or people hold some truth to which others want to attach themselves; it is as if these people or objects can fill a void.

Many people who were raised in neglectful families have learned to be passive, to feel dead inside, and they will often seek out someone or something that makes them feel alive. They tend to give power to and see power in others or in objects, but not in themselves. A client of mine grew up in a neglectful family, and he had a gambling addiction. He explained what he loved about his addiction was how alive he felt when he was doing it. He would put on colorful shirts and look flashy; he'd go to the races and feel alive and sure of himself, after which he had to go back to what he called his, "dull, empty world inside." It was almost as if his addiction allowed him a break from the passiveness he had learned from his family of origin.

Addiction is a relationship issue, and so is neglect. People growing up in a passive, neglectful family are more likely to be followers and to seek out people to tell them how to act. They seek out the life and excitement that was absent while growing up. In addiction there is the mood change, which produces a feeling of self-righteousness and excitement. The Addict often has a cocky, self-righteous quality about it. People growing up in neglectful homes are very susceptible to this false sense of confidence and excitement. They get quite depressed once the acting out is over and their passiveness returns.

Shaming Families

A shaming family is one in which members can never do any-thing right or good enough.

- There are families in which a child comes home with five A's and a B + on his report card, only to get a lecture about how he needs to try harder if he wants to get ahead. "Remember, it is a tough world out there."
- There are families with the disapproving looks, the yes-buts, the put-downs, the long days of total silence for not behaving properly.
- There are families with the constant teasing that almost borders on emotional torture.
- There are families in which a child never feels safe.

Shaming families are families in which members are taught not to take responsibility; shaming families produce large numbers of addicts because they teach children the addictive process. A major byproduct of addiction is shame; another byproduct is not taking responsibility for one's actions and attitudes. Shaming families victimize their members in a routine, systematic way; thus, family members are taught to be either victims or victimizers.

Shaming families set their members up to be emotionally full of rage and at the same time to have a deep sense of sadness. Family members are taught not to be vulnerable, for vulnerability leaves one open for attack. Shaming families push their members to be perfect — perfect angels or perfect sinners. Shaming families teach their members not to be "caught" in the middle, for, being in the middle, according to the attitudes of shaming families, is like standing in the center of a room full of enemies — it means you can be attacked from all sides. Thus, family members back them-selves against a wall and wait to be attacked. People raised in sham-ing families want the seat at the restaurant with its back to the wall; only then do they feel totally safe.

Members of shaming families feel tension in their family system; this often is translated into a general mistrust of human beings.

One of my clients who grew up in a very shame-based family states that the only reason she is here today is because of the care and understanding shown to her by the only family member who would not shame her — the family dog, who was the only family member she could talk with, cry with, and still find him accepting of her. It was interesting that in a family session with her siblings, she found out three of her four siblings reported having an identical relationship with the family dog. This is an example of the great mistrust of people that can be instilled in children who grow up in a shaming family. In this way, members of shaming families can develop a secret life, a secret side to themselves. This helps to push them toward the addictive process. All addicts have a general mistrust of people and have a secret side to themselves. Addicts are involved in behaviors they don't want to tell others about.

To shame someone is to abuse the person, but because it doesn't take the form of yelling, hitting, or sexually abusing the person, it is often seen as acceptable behavior. When family members are around people who come from nonshaming families, there is often a sort of culture shock. They might act with what they think is normal behavior, yet others are appalled. Though we all have been shamed, shaming is not normal — it is tearing someone else down to build oneself up. It is an attack on the person's Self. The most dangerous part of this shaming ritual is that it is almost always done in the disguise of being helpful, or it's done in the name of honesty. The person who puts others to shame will rarely take responsibility for the viciousness of the behavior. As in the earlier example about the report card, the parents would most likely see themselves as trying to be helpful and trying to better their child. If their shaming behavior were pointed out to them, more often they'd refuse to see their own meanness.

Children in shaming families often believe they are bad people and are responsible for their parents' unhappiness. To children, this is the biggest wrong they think they could commit. This becomes their biggest secret — *if people really knew me they wouldn't like me* — and they develop a lifestyle of proving they are bad people or a lifestyle based on keeping their shame a secret from everyone. These are the adults who feel totally crushed or are very defensive if they do anything wrong or if anyone points out a mistake they've made. They are perfect candidates for addiction. They have the deep anger and pain for which relief is needed. They mistrust people and find a comfort in relationships with objects. They've learned not to take responsibility for any of their negative actions; if they did, it would mean, to them, that they were "bad" people. There is a wonderful book on the subject of how families and shame relate to the addiction process. I would highly recommend it to anyone who grew up in an addictive, shaming family. The book is titled, *Facing Shame: Families in Recovery*, by Merle Fossum and Marilyn J. Mason.

Inconsistent Families

Growing up in a family where one or both parents are or act crazy is often like trying to play marbles on the deck of a rolling ship. As rules, behaviors, and views of the world change on a day-to-day basis, there is nothing for the child to attach to and be nurtured by in order to develop. Children need consistency in their lives. In emotionally inconsistent families, what the developing child is deprived of is the opportunity of having a consistent relationship. In some of the other family types we have looked at, there is a consistent relationship; but it may be consistently bad and unhealthy. In the emotionally inconsistent family, a relationship of any depth is never allowed to form — all attempts are sabotaged. People who come from this type of family almost always feel unsure of their social and relationship skills. They tend to be very dependent people. It's as if they get locked into searching for the parents they never had. In this way they are attracted to the consistency found in addiction. Addicts always know where their object is. They are drawn to the assured and confident feeling many addicts feel when acting out, especially in the early stages of the addictive process.

These people are also susceptible to peer pressure. If they end up in a group where being addicted to an object or event is the norm, they are likely to become addicted too.

People raised in inconsistent families seem to have an extremely deep loneliness. They've been taught not to trust or count on people. They crave contact and intimacy with people, but they also mistrust them. As in some other family types, this influences members to have relationships with objects or events in which the illusion of fulfillment is to be found.

Inconsistent parents will often tell their children that their behavior is normal and the rest of the world is crazy. The child is taught not to believe his or her own feelings or intuition. Their feelings might tell them that what is happening in the family is crazy, but their parents continually tell them nothing is wrong. In this way, they are forced to choose between their parents and themselves.

Especially young children in this type of situation will choose their parents' version of reality, for their survival depends on it. This helps them to overlook the inconsistencies found in addiction. A client I worked with came from a very crazy, inconsistent family and he'd talk about how attracted he was to the consistency he found in his alcoholism, and how the periodic crises he had to put up with never worried him too much because they were much less frequent and never had the magnitude of those that were common in his family. He was never too frightened by his periodic blackouts, which didn't compare to coming home to the somewhat routine occurrence of finding his mother trying to kill herself.

Death of a Family Member

I want to remind readers that here, in Part Four of this book, I'm not describing causes of addiction. I have attempted to describe the types of families in which family members seem to have higher rates of addiction. As a clinician I've worked with a lot of addicts who have had a parent die early in their lives or whose parent or sibling was chronically ill while they grew up. While many times the families can be very loving and nurturing, there seems to be something about this type of loss that pushes people toward the addictive process.

Many of these families also have developed a "no talk rule" about the chronic illness or the deceased parent. It is as if the grieving process is not allowed to take place. Consequently, family members are never taught how to express or release their feelings of frustration and loss. Addiction seems to offer a form of release to them, or it offers them an effective way to numb their feelings.

Due to the burden that family members experience in these situations, there may be less positive emotional energy. Especially in families with a chronically ill person, it seems like much of the emotional resources of the family are used in dealing with the illness, much like growing up in an addictive family. Addiction offers these people another way to cope.

PART FIVE

RECOVERY FROM ADDICTION

Some people say that addicts are self-centered. I strongly disagree. Instead, addicts are Addict-centered at a cost to the Self. The process of recovery from the illness of addiction is found in Self-renewal. For us to recover, there has to be a rededication or dedication to Self. In other words, the Self must become important once again.

Recovery is the process of becoming Self-centered. Printed on the medallions that are handed out to recovering addicts on anniversaries of their abstinence are the words: "To Thine Own Self Be True." This is the beginning of recovery: Self-care, and a Self-relationship.

A practicing addict has a relationship between the Self and the Addict; the recovering addict has a relationship between Self and others. What changes? How are the two relationships different? The key ingredient is what's found in any intimate relationship: honesty. The Addict is incapable of honesty, which nurtures and sustains the Self. Thus, it's through honesty that a lasting relationship with Self and others begins and develops. Honesty creates trust and trust creates safety. Recovery is dependent on safety. To grow, we need a safe environment for the Self. Recovering addicts create this safety by honestly and respectfully admitting the danger they are living in. They admit to and claim the addictive personality that is part of them.

"Hi. My name is Mary and I'm an alcoholic."

"Hi. My name is Steve and I'm a sex addict."

"Hi. My name is Julie and I'm an addictive gambler."

At group support meetings, addicts introduce themselves by who they truly are. By honestly admitting they are addicts, they can begin to have a relationship with the Self and other people. Denial, on the other hand, causes the Addict to grow, and the danger to the Self and others increases.

Developing Natural Relationships

Trust is the basis of any relationship, whether the relationship is within oneself or with others. If a relationship is not based on trust, the relationship becomes a struggle. The same is true for the relationship we have with ourselves. Trust allows us the ability to heal and the freedom to connect with others. Twelve Step and other self-help groups need to be safe rest stops where one can go and experience safety. By allowing ourselves to rest and let the healing begin, we can start to relate to people again in a healthy way.

Slowing ourselves down to a human pace is also an essential ingredient for relationships to be formed. Imagine what it would be like to start a conversation with pedestrians from a car that's moving 60 miles per hour. Impossible. But if you slow the car down and stop, you can talk to people outside the car. Most addicts are moving at such great speeds that connecting with anything outside their "vehicles" is impossible. The frightening part is that when addicts look in the rear view mirror, they see their Addict sitting comfortably in the backseat asking the question, "Can't you make this thing go any faster?"

In some cases, recovering addicts need to increase their speed to the pace of the world around them, instead of sitting in a stalled vehicle watching everyone pass by. Recovery is a process of reentering the world.

Reaching Out

Once addicts have gone through the steps of honestly *admitting* and truly *accepting* their illness, they are ready to start forming relationships outside of themselves. It's important to understand that the two steps mentioned must be taken so addicts can make themselves trustworthy to others. If addicts are not safe to be around, most often they'll end up connecting with others who are just as untrustworthy.

Once a safe relationship with ourselves has begun (not established, just begun) the person is ready to start reaching outward. Others may have already been trying to help the addict, but now the addict can do the reaching out for help. He or she can challenge the inward flow of addiction. Whether a person reaches out to family or friends, a Higher Power, or the community is a personal choice. Eventually, recovering addicts need to form intimate relationships with all of these groups, but must first focus on one area.

Spiritual Higher Power

Many begin recovery by going from a relationship with the Self to beginning a relationship with a spiritual Higher Power. In an early stage of recovery, dealing with people is often too frightening. A person's relationship with the Self is still too fragile to form deeply committed relationships with friends or family. Thus, forming a relationship with a spiritual Higher Power is often a natural starting place as the person ventures out into the world.

Recovering addicts start to notice their Higher Power in others. People in recovery often talk about how dangerous they were to themselves and others while actively practicing addiction. They also talk about their relationship with a Higher Power, which has helped to make them trustworthy to others.

In group support meetings, people smile and help each other, wanting nothing more than simple human respect in return. I've always been amazed to watch how observant and attentive new members are as they come into a group. By observing people who exchange dignity with each other, addicts start to sense the presence of a power greater than themselves at work. They start wanting to be a part of this exchange. They start to sense and see themselves as people again, not as objects to be tossed from one crisis to another.

Intimacy

By believing in the healing process, one forms a relationship with a caring Higher Power. Addiction is a power greater than ourselves as most major illnesses are, but recovery is also a power greater than ourselves. The main difference here is that while one is based on dishonesty and destruction, the other is based on care and honesty.

As recovering addicts observe the natural ways in which others nurture themselves, they start to want to have relationships with others on an intimate level. They start to question the addictive belief system that says, "People are not to be trusted" or "You're doomed to be lonely — you're too different — you're not like them." Recovering addicts find they are like others. All of us are unique but also similar, especially within a community of peers. Recovering addicts begin to realize they have found people they can understand, people who are capable of understanding them. Thus, intimate relationships start to make a lot of sense.

Honesty

At about this point, the Addict within the person becomes afraid and starts to tell the person, "These people are phony" or, "Look — see what an angry, controlling person he is? You'd better not trust him." But then the person returns to a meeting the next week and sees these people talking about themselves in a nonshameful way. They recognize and admit to their addictive sides in honest and respectful ways. Self-responsibility is the goal of these people, not denial of responsibility. The honesty of the people around the recovering addict challenges the addictive belief system.

By trusting in the natural healing process, recovering addicts venture outward a little bit more and start sharing things about themselves. The person may be watching and waiting closely (and on the addictive side, hoping) for any put-downs or ridicule. This doesn't happen. Instead, people respond in a natural way. They say, "Oh, yes. I know how that feels. That feels horrible, but it does get better. It's good to see you talking about yourself." People in these groups are working at listening to others. Natural relationships are starting to be formed. Inside, recovering addicts start to feel slightly connected to those who have responded. They start to feel connected to others in the group who share similar experiences.

The Healing Process

Slowly, recovering addicts form relationships that are based on helping others instead of using others. If recovering people do want to use someone, they are clear about it. "I need you to help me stay sober, so please come back" is a statement often heard in group support meetings.

People give each other their phone numbers and say, for example, "If you feel you need to drink, give me a call." Recovering addicts start to feel important again; a sense of self-esteem is formed. They realize they have something to give that can help others. When they walk into meetings, others are happy to see them. Their families are probably glad they're going to meetings, but are still mistrustful of them. People at meetings help everyone realize their families' reactions are natural and logical. "Why should they trust you? They know better than anyone about your Addict and how mean you can be. We do trust you. You've been coming regularly and have been active in meetings, and you look like someone who wants recovery. So, give your family time — they need it." Through this type of dialogue, recovering addicts start to experience natural logic again. What people in the group have to say makes sense and over time everyone sees it work. The group is learning the natural healing process found in honest relationships.

New Values

Through their relationships with other people at meetings, recovering addicts find themselves being renewed. They also start to have a relationship with the principles and concepts found in recovery — principles and concepts such as admitting, accepting, honesty, believing in, letting go, caring, asking for what they need, self-examination, prayer, meditation, and spiritual awakening. All of these principles become part of the recovering addict's Self. Principles such as lying, hiding, and denial had become a part of the Addict. As recovering addicts learn how to have relationships with healthy concepts and principles, the Self is renewed. Recovering addicts start to feel happy and peaceful inside because they are becoming people who deserve respect again. They are being honest people with values that work for them.

Recovery through Respecting the Addiction

As recovering addicts gain strength within, they can begin a process of self-examination that is needed to sustain newly formed relationships and to reclaim relationships that were lost because of the addiction process. As part of this self-examination, recovering addicts are continually forced (in a caring way) to talk about the hell their addiction dragged themselves and their families through. In telling their stories to peers, recovering addicts begin to respect the power of their addiction and the Addict that lives within.

It has been said that a good general may hate the enemy, but will always have a deep respect for the enemy. By repeatedly telling their stories and listening to others, addicts form respect for addiction, enough (it's hoped) to help make them work hard for recovery.

Being Kind to Oneself

In addiction, any form of self-examination ends up being self-abuse. In recovery groups, addicts learn that if they're beating up on themselves, they're still acting like Addicts. They learn to give

94

up this habit by approaching themselves and others with dignity and respect. This is a sober way of living based on recovery; it can be a tough lesson that will take time for many to learn, especially for those who grew up surrounded by addiction.

Monitoring the Addict Within

There are times in recovery when many can still feel and hear the Addict within. If the Addict starts to get too loud or sound too good, recovering addicts can go to their new relationships and the safety they have found in them. Addiction is "cunning, baffling, powerful!" The Addict doesn't simply give up. Most often, the Addict sits there and makes sullen comments that are well thought out and cause self-doubt.

One of the things people need to do throughout recovery is monitor their Addict. The Addict within will look for other objects or events to form an addictive relationship.

- Recovering alcoholics may find themselves, after two or three years, being 50 or 60 pounds overweight.
- Recovering sex addicts may start drinking or going to the racetrack too often.
- Addictive gamblers may start having a few drinks when they gamble.
- Sex addicts may start using laxatives on a regular basis to regulate their weight.

This is part of the "cunning" aspect of addiction that all recovering addicts need to watch out for. The Addict within has a favorite addiction, but other ways will do. Secondary addictions can become primary addictions if a person doesn't monitor the Addict.

The Danger of Switching Addictions

Too much emphasis can be placed on the object of addiction. Addicts in recovery will need to examine not only why they choose a particular object of addiction, they will also need to examine how they interact with the world in addictive ways. They will need to examine their addictive logic, their addictive beliefs, values, and addictive rituals. They need to continually examine these issues until they get to know the addictive side of themselves and have ways to counteract their addictive impulses.

In the Big Book, *Alcoholics Anonymous*, there is a phrase that says, "We feel that the elimination of our drinking is but a beginning." Recovery is not only about stopping acting out, it is also about eliminating the addictive personality that is developed during addiction. If people don't claim and change their addictive personalities, most likely they'll return to some form of acting out. They may have learned enough not to go back to their object of preference, but they may find another object that can help them achieve the mood change needed to escape from unpleasant and unwanted emotions. If addicts don't deal with their addictive personalities and they happen to switch objects of addiction, there is a greater possibility of them returning to their object or event of preference.

In the alcoholism treatment field there is the term "dry drunk" to describe people who have stopped drinking but have not dealt with their addictive personalities. They walk around unhappy, treating everyone the way they did when they were drinking. Thus, recovery is not just about breaking off one's relationship with an object or event, though this is of great importance. Recovery is primarily about coming to know one's addictive personality and taking the necessary steps to rid oneself of addictive attitudes, beliefs, values, and behaviors.

Dry drunks have a greater chance of drinking again. They also have a greater likelihood of switching objects of addiction. Maybe they'll stop drinking but gain 50 or 60 pounds, eating junk food at times when they would have gotten drunk before. They can get away with this because it's more acceptable in our culture to have a food addiction than a drinking addiction. Their lives and relationships might be in shambles, but many will say "at least they're not drinking." While this is true, they are still living an addictive lifestyle and are in danger of drinking again.

People switch addictions to keep the addictive process going. Addicts may get into trouble with one object; to correct the problem they switch to a different object or event. It is much the same as getting out of one bad marriage and jumping into another. One client I was working with had been married four times. Each time his spouse was an addict: two alcoholics, one food addict, and one sex addict who kept having affairs throughout the marriage. This pattern continued until he admitted what he gained from choosing addicts for partners: a sense of superiority. He grew up with a mother who was alcoholic, and addictive logic was the only logic he had learned. By being with someone who was always in trouble, his own problems were never dealt with. He admitted he was scared to be in an equal relationship. It was not until he admitted and accepted these and other parts of himself that he was able to establish different types of relationships.

I remember doing an evaluation with a man who reported that he once had a whiskey problem. He gave up whiskey, then started to develop a problem with gin. He gave up gin. He then developed a problem with wine and had to give it up. When I saw him he was questioning the way he was using beer, and wanted to talk to someone before he became an alcoholic.

Addicts switch objects of addiction in order to continue the addictive process and the illusion that they don't have a problem. Addicts are seeking the mood change and often how they get it is of little importance.

How do recovering addicts know if they're starting to act out addictively with other objects or events? If they start to use other objects or events to replace relationships or the principles of a recovery program, they are starting to act in an addictive manner. If they become secretive about their behaviors, they are probably starting to use objects or events addictively. When recovering addicts act secretive about their behaviors, they start to cut themselves off from the natural helping and healing process. They start to isolate themselves.

If recovering addicts start to feel bad about certain behaviors and don't talk about these with others within their support system, they are starting to act in an addictive manner again. They prevent themselves from the healing that takes place when they talk about their issues with others. By talking with others about their behaviors, recovering addicts can see their actions are either normal and helpful, or addictive and dangerous. Most people in recovery come to accept that their Addict will always be with them and that they can effectively monitor addiction with the help of a recovery program. They accept that their illness has changed them in some permanent ways, as all major illnesses do. Addicts can recover, but are never cured.

Honesty and Recovery

For recovery to be genuine, at some time the recovering person must dedicate his or her life to achieving honesty, which is opposite addiction. Honesty must be the backbone of one's recovery program. To recover, one has to admit to the existence of a problem and then be honest about the need for help. Honesty is the beginning of recovery and is also the fuel that keeps recovery going.

Practicing addicts fear honesty. Recovering addicts may not always like honesty, but they accept honest criticism and learn to turn their weaknesses into strengths.

Honesty is especially important to recovering addicts because it counteracts the addictive process. The denial and dishonesty in addiction causes people to become more distant from themselves and others. Dishonesty eventually causes isolation; most often, only the addict knows he or she is being dishonest, and is forced inward and away from others.

Honesty is about connecting with ourselves and others; it allows us to have intimate relationships. Honesty doesn't always guarantee intimacy, but it allows a relationship to connect more fully.

Honesty toward oneself or others must include understanding and compassion. As a therapist, I've seen a lot of cruel things done in the name of honesty, and because of this I've come to believe honesty shouldn't include cruelty. Honesty and revenge have nothing in common.

Honesty takes place on the inside; it can then be directed outward. Honesty is not about finding someone to blame, though in addiction systems it is often seen this way. Honesty is mainly about how one views the world and sharing this with others. In this way, honesty is about how we as individuals differ from each other. What is honest for me can be and most likely is different from what is honest for you. This is because we all have different backgrounds and perspectives. Thus, honesty is really about self-monitoring and then sharing ourselves with others.

If we are trying to be honest we will spend little, if any, time trying to figure out if others are being honest, which is most often a waste of time. If someone is generally a dishonest person, this will be revealed; dishonesty, like honesty, is a lifestyle. A truly dishonest lifestyle creates discrepancies, and as the dishonesty goes on these discrepancies will become obvious until they become public. This is what happens in addiction.

Honest people work to be open and genuine. They are proud of themselves in a very genuine way. They want to know themselves better so they can improve. Recovering addicts need to embrace the concept of honesty because it allows them to continue recovery. By being honest, recovering people will allow themselves to seek help when they want to act out. By being honest, recovering people become aware of their own issues early enough to do something about them before they become excuses to act out.

Honesty has a frankness to it. This is found when people introduce themselves in many self-help groups. "Hi, my name is _____ and I'm an addict." This kind of honesty is a starting point. The person represents him- or herself without any fraud or shame.

Honesty is free of judgment and blame. It may hold guilt but no shame. It is about facts — personal facts. "I see things this way," or, "I believe things to be that way." Honesty is an act of sharing one's beliefs and ideas with others or with oneself in a nonjudgmental way. The good or bad of the issue is left out.

Honesty is also an act of growth — it changes as we change. What seems true today may not be true tomorrow. As we wrestle with issues of honesty we are forced to grow and face our own discrepancies. To be honest is to not dismiss personal inconsistencies when we encounter them. Honesty is to look inward and, at times, outward to discover our beliefs and values.

Honesty is hard for most of us to learn because throughout our lives we are taught certain kinds of dishonesty, especially with our emotions. "Big boys don't cry." "Girls don't get angry." These are two examples of lies we learn. These aren't truths — they're opinions. Most often we are given others' personal beliefs and told these beliefs are facts. Most people get into trouble when they try to get others to believe that their personal opinions are facts. It's easy to think we know all about a person or we know what's best for that person. This is especially easy to do in relationships, but isn't always helpful. If we try to convince people that we know them better than they know themselves, most often all we'll get in return is resentment.

In addiction, people become dedicated to a dishonest lifestyle. In early recovery, people often feel the urge to be dishonest, but their recovery programs tell them to abandon old beliefs and to be honest and trust in people.

Honesty is hard work for most people in early recovery. It's like learning a new language. Once we become familiar with the new language of honesty, it starts to be fun and exciting and starts to feel normal.

Many in early recovery believe honesty means telling all to everyone, but honesty doesn't mean telling our life story to someone we just met on the bus. There's a selectiveness about honesty, and this takes time to develop. Honesty is about sharing ourselves with others, but we would be foolish to do this with some people. We wouldn't tell a burglar our address, and we wouldn't give the burglar anyone else's address either. Honesty, when shared with someone we trust, is a gift.

Most of recovery is about honesty with oneself, which leads to self-acceptance. In recovery, people learn they are the victims of their own lies. To recover, people have to give up the myth of perfection. Most people become dishonest because of this myth. If you believe you have to be perfect, you become dishonest when you deny your imperfections. If there seem to be too many imperfections, you might give up hope. In recovery, people learn to work toward progress, not perfection. They learn it's all right to be imperfect and to be honest with themselves and others about this.

Honesty and acceptance of ourselves gives us self-dignity. Recovery and honesty allows people a life they can be proud of, and allows them to step away from the shame surrounding addiction.

Honesty is also about seeing the world as it is. We live in a beautiful but also ugly world. Honesty can motivate us to see things realistically. By seeing things as they truly are, some are sickened enough to try to change things. A recovering person is someone who is reclaiming personal power. Addicts know much about being powerless, being caught up in a disease that has controlled them. Recovering addicts learn much about empowerment and how, by being connected with others and with a loving spirit, they can bring about changes in their lives.

Relationships and Recovery

The beauty of recovery is found in relationships. It's through forming healthy relationships that addicts are able to overcome their illness. Here, I want to restate my definition of addiction: *Addiction is a pathological love and trust relationship with an object or event.* Recovering addicts must dedicate themselves to learning how to get their love, trust, and emotional needs met through healthy relationships with other people and their own spirituality.

For many recovering people, the first fulfilling relationships they develop are in self-help groups. Many of these self-help groups are based on the Twelve Steps of Alcoholics Anonymous. The first word of the First Step in any of these Twelve Step programs (for example, Families Anonymous, Emotions Anonymous, Overeaters Anonymous, or Narcotics Anonymous*) is what I be-

---

*There are over 100 different kinds of Twelve Step programs active at the present time throughout the world.

lieve to be the most important word of all: "We." By using the word "We," the Twelve Steps start to break the unhealthy relationship between the Addict and Self and start to connect the Self with others. As this happens, people realize their emotional needs can be attained through other people. If the unhealthy relationship between Addict and Self is not broken and replaced by healthy relationships with others, addicts will most often return to an addiction or replace the addiction with another addictive relationship with an object or event.

In recovery, people need to develop healthy relationships with other recovering addicts, the spiritual side of themselves, family and friends, and eventually the community they live in. It is in these natural relationships that people come to know themselves and learn to meet emotional needs in nonaddictive ways. It is through others that recovering addicts develop the skills of feeling comfortable and enjoying themselves.

In the beginning of the recovery process, relationships are often viewed as something not to be trusted. In the addiction process, addicts use people as objects. The healing powers found in healthy relationships will start to comfort addicts. This is most often what addicts have wanted all along: comforting relationships. Almost all people crave relationships that comfort and nurture them, relationships in which they feel important and proud to be a part of.

Addicts often believe they are incapable of having relationships that work. They have tried, but their relationships never seem to work out. Their relationships can't work because of the addictive process. Eventually, addicts end up seeing themselves as unlovable. In forming healthy, intimate relationships we discover our ability to love and be loved. It's through these relationships that we experience ourselves as special.

People start to come alive as they develop relationships. Recovering addicts will often do almost anything to help other addicts recover. I've seen the biggest and roughest looking men gently hold a shaky member of their group and allow the person to cry on their shoulders, telling the person he has nothing to fear anymore, for he now has friends.

In relationships we learn how to deal with the issues of life. Most major issues in life are worked out in the context of relationships. Some basic elements of a healthy relationship are:

1. Showing respectful behavior toward another person.
2. Feeling supported by another person.
3. Being accepted for who you are and not for what someone else would like you to be.
4. Caring about nurturing the humanity of the other person.

Respectful Behavior for Others

In a relationship, one needs to treat the other person as being important because that person is a human being. One needs to work to create a feeling of safety, and respect helps achieve this. Respect helps to build trust in a relationship with others and with oneself. If people treat themselves and others in a respectful manner, they start to trust and believe in themselves.

For any relationship to work, there has to be mutual respect. This respect has to be expressed in both words and actions. It's not enough to say you respect another person. You must *act* in respectful ways.

If a person is thought to be respectful, it is a statement about how that person acts. It is a statement about how the person tries to interact with others. It speaks of honesty. Honesty based on respect is how we give others dignity and shows how we are being honest about ourselves to others. But respect is not just about being honest; it's also about the manner in which we are honest — being honest with dignity toward the others.

Feeling Supported

Within a healthy relationship there is active support for the other person. Each person will work at helping the other get what he or she needs and wants out of life. In this way each person is involved with the other's life, asking questions to find out what is important in that person's life.

In many relationships, there is much talk of support but little evidence of it. In a healthy relationship, the talk is always followed by action. People don't feel used; they feel valued and important in the eyes of others. Because of this there is little mistrust.

A major way we support another person in a relationship is by keeping the person safe from our own nastiness. All of us have meanness inside of us. In supportive relationships people don't tear at each other physically or verbally. We may feel like getting mean, but in a healthy relationship we choose the relationship over any momentary sense of power we might think we get from being mean to the other person. We work at having a powerful relationship instead of having power over another person. This isn't to say that in healthy relationships people don't fight, but they argue by rules of mutual respect. Arguments end up settling issues instead of creating them. In addiction, disagreements are a way to try and get one's own way or to get one's point across rather than to settle issues.

Being Accepted for Who You Are

In a healthy relationship, it's understood that it's insane to attempt to have control over another person because it leads to distance and resentments. Trying to control another person creates an "I am better than you" type of interaction. "Because I'm better than you, I get to have control over you." This is the type of logic found in addiction. These types of relationships end up as power struggles, often with the loudest and meanest person having the most power.

In healthy relationships, individual differences are respected and celebrated. The differences and the different views of the world are seen as assets, not liabilities. Thus, each person's strengths are respected and sought out when needed. The leadership within the relationship changes as different skills and abilities are needed to solve issues that confront the relationship.

In a healthy relationship, there is no attempt to reshape the other person into some image that we have of what is "best" for him or her. It is accepted that each person is an expert on him- or herself and that it is impossible to know someone better than the person knows oneself.

Defining Abstinence in Recovery

I am a firm believer in total abstinence. Defining total abstinence is easier in some addictions than in others. For example, it is easier to define total abstinence in addictions that deal with alcohol and other drugs, or an event like gambling. It's harder to define abstinence in some of the other addictions like food, sex, shopping, money, or work. You can't expect people to be nonsexual or ask them never to eat again.

Thus, defining abstinence will consist of defining addictive behaviors and rituals used in the process of acting out. The person will need to commit to being abstinent from these behaviors and rituals. Recovering addicts need to be very clear and specific and totally honest with themselves and others when deciding what is addictive behavior for them. Some people relapse because they define abstinence too loosely.

- Sex addicts may tell themselves it's not okay to see prostitutes, but they still allow themselves to view movies with strong sexual content, while knowing that this may provoke their addiction.

Some people make their definitions of abstinence too rigid, as if to punish themselves — this might be done out of shame. This also will not work. Most often the person will eventually become angry at these overly tight restrictions and rebel against them. This is why it is very important to develop a realistic abstinence contract.

Planning an abstinence contract is something not to be done alone. It is best done with a counselor, a sponsor, or another person with a stable recovery. Many involved in Twelve Step programs place a lot of importance on sponsorship. The idea is to have someone in a safe environment help you decide exactly what objects or events you used that led to addiction, and what behaviors would create a mood change.

- For the alcoholic, abstinence may not only mean not drinking, it may also mean not going to bars, not traveling alone for a period of time, and not going to cocktail parties.

Abstinence means not only avoiding the object of one's addiction, but also defining all the events that added to the addiction process, and developing strategies to protect oneself from these events and behaviors.

Defining abstinence is a process of examining one's addictive rituals that cause or add to a mood change. Defining these rituals can be a dangerous step in recovery because of the danger of preoccupation. In thinking a lot about what it is that excites the Addict, the person can reenter the addictive process. This is why it's important for the person to settle on a definition with someone who knows about addiction and has the time to be with and help the person through any difficulties.

Once addicts have defined what abstinence means to them, they need to publicly share this information with everyone they have chosen to help them stay abstinent. While talking about this subject with a support system, people's abstinence contract will become clear and more real to them. This abstinence contract should be reevaluated periodically, especially in the first year of recovery, adding to it any behaviors that may endanger recovery.

Guilt Versus Shame in Recovery

Because addiction creates and instills shame, many people enter recovery with a deep sense of shame about some of the things they've done during their addiction. Others who enter recovery may not feel any shame, believing there is nothing wrong about what they've done. Somewhere in their recovery process, however, these people often go through a period of feeling very shameful as they look more honestly at their actions of the past.

Addiction is about shame. The more shame, the better for the addictive process. Shame tends to trap people in one of two ways:

(1) people can end up feeling so depressed they start to believe there is nothing they can do about their problems; (2) people can become very self-defensive as they try to escape from their internal sense of shame. They become consumed by their defenses. They can't hear or let anyone in. Oftentimes, these are the people who have bought the myth that they have to be perfect.

Recovery is not about shame. Shame judges one's actions and looks to convict the person for being unworthy. Shame becomes a judgment against the person rather than against the person's actions. Shame is all-consuming.

Recovery does, however, make room for guilt. Recovering people need to learn the difference between guilt and shame. Guilt allows for correcting (or at least thinking about) the offending action. It allows people to regain their dignity and sense of self-respect. In contrast, shame allows none of this to happen.

Guilt means you have committed an action that was wrong or not helpful to others or to yourself. Shame means you are wrong. With guilt, if you have acted in a nonhelpful way, you're allowed to correct the action and all will be forgiven and forgotten. In shame there is no forgiveness, and nothing is forgotten. Shaming families can have the same fight going on for years and years.

Recovery is a process of admitting one's addiction and powerlessness over that addiction. Recovery is a process of surrendering to realities of the past and present. Recovery is a process of claiming responsibility for one's actions. Responsibility is a cornerstone of recovery. Recovering addicts are guilty of having an illness; they are guilty of being and acting like addicts. All of this must be admitted. It can be difficult to admit these issues without falling into shame.

Recovering addicts must claim responsibility for their past actions, but they must also avoid becoming shameful about their actions. They may feel bad about the ways they have acted and about those they have hurt. This is part of recovery; it is part of having a conscience. But they need to stay away from convicting themselves as being bad people.

During their addiction, most addicts feel so shameful that shame becomes familiar. They don't like it, but it's helpful to the addictive process: if they think they are bad people, then they conclude they are not responsible for their actions because bad people act in bad ways. This is addictive logic.

Because of this, recovering addicts need to change their perspective of themselves. Instead of seeing themselves as bad people, they need to see themselves as people who have an illness that causes them to act in addictive ways. The illness can't be cured, but it can be treated if the people with the illness are willing to work for recovery. They still are responsible for the pain and anger they have caused, but now they have a starting place from which they can recover: they realize that they aren't bad people; instead, they realize they have done bad things to others, and this affects their conscience. Shame doesn't allow a person to recover.

Shameful people continue to act in bad ways, at least occasionally, in order to convince themselves that they are bad people. These are the ones in recovery programs who occasionally are screwing up and sounding like martyrs. Internally, they continue to see themselves as bad people.

Guilt teaches people to take responsibility for their actions. Much of the recovery process is based on this. Recovering addicts learn to monitor their actions, and when they act in nonhelpful ways they do not become shameful or hide or get defensive; they admit to their behavior and make amends.

Making amends does not mean saying, "I'm sorry." It means recognizing and thinking, *because of how I acted, there is an inequality in our relationship. Now I need to find out from the person I hurt what is needed for the relationship to become equal again.*

- If a person, during his addiction, had continually yelled and blown up at his spouse, making amends would not just mean saying, "I'm sorry." It would mean admitting to his spouse, "I've done this and I've done that which I know has caused you great pain and frustration." Then asking the question, "What do you need from me to make up for this?"

Then he would do what his spouse has said (within realistic limits, for addicts made some people very angry) as an act of restitution.

Thus, through claiming responsibility for their actions, recovering addicts may gain back some of the relationships lost due to their addiction. We are all human and we'll all act like jerks from time to time. Guilt teaches people how to see themselves through realistic eyes, but shame is a distortion of reality.

Rituals and Recovery

Rituals are as important to the recovery process as they are to the addictive process. Recovering people will need to develop positive, self-enriching rituals. These rituals must be of the type that help connect them with other recovering people, to the principles of recovery, to their own spiritual centers, and to the spirits of others around them. Positive rituals are about connection, identification, commitment, and about the fact that all of us need to be connected to something. Addictive rituals are mostly about separation; rituals of recovery are about connection.

Many of the people I've worked with have a simple ritual of reading about recovery each morning or evening and then meditating on what they have just read. This personal ritual ties them to the recovery process. It allows them to commit themselves to recovery on a daily basis.

Recovery is about choices; addiction is about not having choices. Recovering people need to and do continually choose recovery. Rituals of recovery are behaviors that help people exercise their choices. Rituals need to be both public and private, just as addiction is both public and private. In rituals, people engage in routine and consistent behaviors. By developing rituals of recovery, recovering addicts will routinely bind themselves to new beliefs and values that are opposite of those found in addiction. Thus, they bind themselves to a process of growth; they commit themselves to caring and nurturing themselves and others. Rituals are statements, a form of language, an act of commitment. Through rituals, recovering addicts learn to develop and commit to a language and lifestyle of self-care.

As people in recovery develop their own rituals of recovery, they are learning to act in certain ways. Recovery does have a code of conduct: You are to treat yourself and others in a respectful and nurturing way. You are to help yourself and others whenever help is needed, if it can be done in a nurturing way. This code of conduct is found in the rituals of recovery. Taking time to reflect, taking time to visit and listen to others, praying on a regular basis in any style one chooses, are all behaviors that become ritualized in recovery. All rituals of recovery are based on binding the person to the parts of our world from which we get healing, nurturing, and love.

As time goes on, the recovering person will find much comfort in the rituals of recovery. I was working with a client who was involved in a Twelve Step program. She had to do some traveling for her business that involved going to a couple of different foreign countries. She went to Twelve Step meetings in those countries and found much comfort and serenity as she engaged in the same rituals as her home group thousands of miles away. She didn't understand the language foreign members of the Twelve Step groups were speaking, but she totally understood their rituals of recovery. She was able to find comfort and nurturing in the predictability of these rituals, while renewing her commitment to recovery.

Rituals are about faith, about life. By engaging in rituals, recovering addicts connect themselves to others and start to have faith in people and themselves again. By turning to their rituals in times of stress recovering addicts are able to reduce the personal stress they feel inside.

Recovery as a Community

Many come to depend in a healthy way on the "we" of a recovery program. It is through the "we" of the group process that people feel confident they can recover from their illness, not by themselves but within a recovering community.

It makes a lot of sense that "we" is the first word in the First Step of any Twelve Step program. Recovering addicts find comfort in the presence of other people, instead of being afraid of them. They start to become we-centered instead of addiction-centered. They consider whether their friends would favor a certain behavior or action. They make decisions on how to act by asking themselves whether or not they would feel good talking about it with friends. They borrow a collective conscience until they develop a personal conscience that works for them. In other words, they learn to have an interdependent relationship with their community.

Instead of feeling totally alone in the world, recovering addicts begin to see themselves as part of a worldwide community. They become not only part of a Twelve Step community, but a part of the community they live in. They learn to be citizens — first as citizens of a Twelve Step community, and then as citizens of the larger community. They may do volunteer work, donate to worthy projects, talk to their neighbors, and vote. They sense the "we" inside of them and are glad to be a part of the world again.

- A recovering addict is volunteering to do things for his community. Where did he learn this? Perhaps it all started the time he volunteered to come early to a meeting and make coffee for his group. He remembers how good that felt. He remembers the words of the Twelve Step program that you can't keep anything you don't give away. He remembers the stories of the founding members of Alcoholics Anonymous who, whenever the urge to drink occurred, would try to help other alcoholics in need. He has learned that by helping others a person helps him- or herself to be human.

Thus, over time the "we" of the program expands to the surrounding community and to the world.

Sometime during the recovery process, it is hoped that family and friends start to trust the recovering addict. Regaining trust in a recovering addict will happen sooner if family and friends become involved in looking at how addiction has affected them. It's equally important that recovering addicts begin treating their families and friends with dignity. If they don't treat their families and friends with dignity and respect, they aren't practicing recovery.

It is through personal relationships that addicts get the day-to-day practice of how to be respectful, recovering people. It's easy to do this once or twice a week at meetings, but permanent healing takes place when recovering addicts learn, practice, and adopt respectful attitudes in their own homes, in their work, and when they are by themselves. A recovering addict may wish to ask him- or herself, "Am I acting in a way I would be comfortable talking about with my friends?" "Am I listening to family members with as much understanding as I listen to members of my group?"

Addiction attacks family relationships with great intensity because it's here where a deep, lasting intimacy can be cultivated. It's here where love and respect become more than just words. It's within a family where one finds his or her true Self. It's within the family where the Self either develops or does not grow. It's here that recovery becomes a lifestyle.

It's through becoming respectful members of a family that the circle from addiction to recovery is completed. This can be a very hard task. Most often within a family there is much anger, fear, and mistrust due to a person's addiction. Old behavior patterns will tempt a recovering addict. There may be others in a family who are practicing addicts and refuse to treat a recovering family member with respect. No matter how they are treated or looked upon by others, recovering addicts need to learn to nurture others within the context of a family. They also need to be themselves within the context of the family. In doing these things, recovering addicts learn self-responsibility, and recovery becomes a day-to-day program. When recovery occurs in such a way, many feel their spirits awaken. When recovering addicts realize they are able to have relationships with the Self, a spiritual Higher Power, friends, family, and their community, they feel complete. They feel the full healing power of relationships. They have acquired what a recovery program and relationships are all about.

A recovering person's goal is to become expert in having meaningful relationships. A recovery program and the principles and fellowship found there give recovering addicts a foundation in learning to have meaningful relationships. Through daily practice of these principles, they acquire the discipline within themselves to have respectful relationships.

Recovering addicts can choose the work of recovery from which they will learn to discipline themselves, or they can choose not to become disciplined. In order to have relationships with the Self, a spiritual Higher Power, family, friends, and community, recovering addicts need to choose to become disciplined. By "disciplined," I do not mean in a tough, hard way (the addictive way), but in a concerned, compassionate way. Recovery is a choice and a privilege. To be given the power of choice is a beautiful aspect in recovery. When addicts choose to become recovering people and behave as recovering people, they are teaching themselves about self-responsibility, self-care, and self-nurturing.

It is written in one of the scriptures: "I give you life. I give you death. Choose life." This is what recovery from addiction is all about.

INDEX